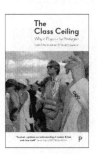

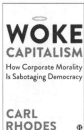

Find out more at bristoluniversitypress.co.uk

 **BRISTOL UNIVERSITY PRESS**

Home of  **Policy Press**

Our series and journals include:

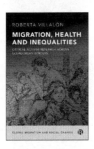

Find out more at bristoluniversitypress.co.uk

GLOBAL AGENDA FOR SOCIAL JUSTICE 2

Edited by
Glenn W. Muschert, Kristen M. Budd,
Heather Dillaway, David C. Lane,
Manjusha Nair, and Jason A. Smith

First published in Great Britain in 2022 by

Policy Press, an imprint of
Bristol University Press
University of Bristol
1-9 Old Park Hill
Bristol
BS2 8BB
UK
t: +44 (0)117 374 6645
e: bup-info@bristol.ac.uk

Details of international sales and distribution partners are available at
policy.bristoluniversitypress.co.uk

British Library Cataloguing in Publication Data
A catalogue record for this book is available from the British Library

ISBN 978-1-4473-6740-6 paperback
ISBN 978-1-4473-6741-3 ePub
ISBN 978-1-4473-6742-0 ePdf

Cover design: Hayes Design and Advertising
Front cover image: Brush rainbow circle © Iona/Freepik
Bristol University Press and Policy Press use environmentally responsible print partners.
Printed in Great Britain by CMP, Poole

Table of contents

President's welcome

Noreen Sugrue

The members of the Society for the Study of Social Problems (SSSP) are scholars who conduct cutting-edge research and, as activists and advocates, use that research to fight for a better, fairer world for all. The work done by members of the SSSP is needed now more than ever.

SSSP members are needed to identify and analyze, as well as offer solutions to, problems that are endemic across the globe. These problems include such issues as racism, sexism, criminal justice reform, immigration, refugee resettlement, and Lesbian, Gay, Bisexual, Trans, Queer/Questioning, Asexual, and Intersex (LGBTQAI) equity, to name but a few. In addition, SSSP members also prioritize working on wealth inequality, as well as the looming existential crisis of climate change.

Each member of the SSSP is called upon, required really, to assist in creating and sustaining more equitable and just social orders. In *Global Agenda for Social Justice 2*, an impressive array of SSSP scholars do exactly that. They are the embodiment of what all SSSP members do each day in their lives—they offer identification and analysis of an array of problems but then take their responsibility and work a step further by offering a guide for how to actually solve those problems. Embedded in those solutions are the ingredients that, when taken together, will forge the fundamental and systemic change required to have a fairer, as well as a more just and equitable, world order.

It is those actions of incubating social change through data-driven research and advocacy that set the SSSP apart from other organizations. It is the foundation on which the organization is built, and it is that foundation on which *Global Agenda for Social Justice 2* sits. I encourage each of you to follow the lead of the volume's authors and begin building a pathway to constructing and implementing workable solutions to our most pressing social problems.

It is with a debt of gratitude for pushing each of us to continue in the storied tradition of scholar advocates and activists that I thank Glenn W. Muschert, as well as the other editors and all of the authors of *Global Agenda for Social Justice 2*. I thank them for continuing to push each of us to conduct quality research and advocate for changes that will lead to a more just and moral world.

Through the writings in *Global Agenda for Social Justice 2*, each of us is challenged to elevate the commitments and ideals on which the SSSP was founded and continues to thrive. All involved in *Global Agenda for Social Justice 2* are helping to redefine and shape both the narrative around and solutions to social problems; they do this by infusing their findings, ideas, and solutions into the policy process.

Editorial introduction

*Glenn W. Muschert, Kristen M. Budd, Heather Dillaway,
David C. Lane, Manjusha Nair, and Jason A. Smith*

This volume is the latest from a project called Justice 21, inspired by the 2000 presidential address delivered by Professor Robert Perrucci, the 48th President of the SSSP. Dr Perrucci cautioned that SSSP members and other social scientists were losing focus on their mandate to study pressing social problems in order to generate solutions to reduce or abolish them (Perrucci, 2001). He warned that as sociology and related disciplines became more inwardly academic in focus, they became less relevant in public discourse, social action, and policy regimes. He reminded us that our role, to paraphrase Karl Marx, was not merely to study society (and its problems), but also to change it (for the better) (Engels, 1988: 69–72).

To overcome this problem and reorient social problems research, Dr Perrucci called upon the SSSP to produce a "report to the nation," the launch of which would precede US presidential elections. Chapters in the report were to be brief (about 3,000 words), jargon-free, and accessible to intelligent, nonacademic readers. Each chapter would focus on a concrete social problem, following a three-part structure: (1) definition of the problem; (2) outline of evidence about the problem; and (3) concrete solutions to reduce or solve the problem.

To achieve this vision, the SSSP established an ad hoc committee known as Justice 21 that was responsible for the publication of the *Agenda for Social Justice*. In 2004 and 2008, the SSSP self-published hard copies of the volumes, as well as e-book and print-on-demand versions in 2012. In 2016, the SSSP partnered with the Policy Press, an academic publisher based at the University of Bristol (UK). The Policy Press espouses a vision congruent with the SSSP mission, including "to encourage problem-centered social research and to foster cooperative relations among persons and organizations engaged in the application of scientific sociological findings to the formulation of social policies" (Society for the Study of Social Problems, 2022). Thus, the partnership between the Policy Press and the Justice 21 Committee (and the SSSP more broadly) has been fruitful, as both organizations pursue public sociology in the pursuit of social justice. The Justice 21 committee further partnered with the Policy Press in 2018 to publish the first *Global Agenda for Social Justice*, whose focus was transnational or global. In 2020, the group published another (US focused) volume in the *Agenda for Social Justice* series and two rapid-response volumes on the impact of COVID-19 in the social problems fields.

The current volume is the second of the global-focuses books in the *Global Agenda for Social Justice* series. The volume contains 11 topical chapters, focusing on a pressing global social problem's definition, extent, and solution. The volume also concludes with three reflective pieces: two "think pieces" that discuss aspects of how scholars might fruitfully conceptualize global social problems and one "action piece" that addresses the issue of "What is to be done?" Our contributors bring a wide range of perspectives, but each brings to the table academic insights generated via rigorous scholarship to develop practicable policies to mitigate or eliminate social problems. In all, 32 scholars from eight countries—Germany, Ghana, New Zealand, Norway, the Russian Federation, the United Arab Emirates, the UK, and the US—contributed as authors and editors. Contributors include those in public policy and advocacy roles, as well as academics at various career stages, ranging from graduate students to faculty members at all ranks, for example, assistant, associate, full, and emeritus professor ranks. Among the contributors are past presidents of the SSSP and the International Sociological Association. Contributor biographical sketches appear in the volume; however, space does not allow a voluminous list of publications produced by our contributors.

Generally, those engaged in social science research and public sociology wish to remain somewhat dispassionate about social problems, as we do not wish our emotions or outrage to obfuscate our communication. On the other hand, each contributor has a long-standing professional commitment to fixing social problems. Each colleague also deeply cares about the problems they study and those who suffer from their effects. Such commitment lies close to the heart of the Justice 21 project and indeed the broader SSSP membership. Each chapter in this volume can stand on its own. Therefore, it is possible to select any chapter for reading and discussion in classrooms, cafes, or community venues concerning social problems. The list of topics discussed in the volume is broad and varied but is by no means intended to be comprehensive of all significant social problems in the world.

The team on the Justice 21 committee hope that this volume as a whole will provide information and great utility to students, policymakers, researchers, and the general public. Please take the enclosed research, arguments, and solutions into debates in classrooms and other venues, using them as a point of discussion among peers to share our vision of social justice to inspire corrective actions for global social problems. We welcome our readers wholeheartedly and look forward to creating more inclusive, equitable, healthy, peaceful, and just societies worldwide.

References

Engels, F. (1888) *Ludwig Feuerbach und der Ausgang der Klassischen deutschen Philosophie ... Mit Anhang Karl Marx über Feuerbach von Jahre 1845* [*Ludwig Feuerbach and the End of Classical German Philosophy ... with Notes on Feuerbach by Karl Marx 1845*]. Berlin: Verlag von J.H.W. Dietz.

Perrucci, R. (2001) Inventing social justice: SSSP and the twenty-first century. *Social Problems*, 48(2): 159–67. Available at: https://doi.org/10.1525/sp.2001.48.2.159

Society for the Study of Social Problems (2022) *SSSP By-Laws*, The Society for the Study of Social Problems. Available at: https://www.sssp1.org/index.cfm/m/29/locationSectionId/0/By-Laws

About the SSSP

The SSSP (Society for the Study of Social Problems) is an academic and action-oriented professional association, whose purpose is to promote and protect social science research and teaching about significant social problems in society. Members of the SSSP include students, faculty members at educational institutions, researchers, practitioners, and advocates.

Some of the SSSP's core activities include encouraging rigorous research, nurturing young sociologists, focusing on solutions to the problems of society, and fostering cooperative relations between the academic and the policy and/or social action spheres. To learn more about joining the SSSP, reading our publications, or attending our annual conference, please visit the SSSP website (available at: www.sssp1.org).

Finally, please consider supporting the SSSP, a nonprofit 501(c)3 organization that accepts tax-deductible contributions both in support of its general operations and for specific purposes. It is possible to donate to the SSSP in general, but it is also possible to donate in support of specific efforts. If you would like to encourage the kind of public sociology represented in this book, please consider supporting the efforts of the Justice 21 committee. For information on contributing, please visit: www.sssp1.org/index.cfm/m/584/.

Notes on contributors

Margaret Abraham is a professor of sociology and the Harry H. Wachtel Distinguished Professor at Hofstra University, USA. She is a past president of the International Sociological Association (2014–18). Her teaching and research interests include social justice, gender, ethnicity, citizenship, globalization, migration, intersectionality, and domestic violence. Margaret has been involved in research and activism for over three decades, has several publications, and has given talks across the world. She serves on community board organizations and journal editorial boards, and is an advisory board member on projects addressing gender-based violence. She has been honored for her work by community-based and academic organizations.

Madelaine Adelman earned a PhD in cultural anthropology at Duke University. She is a professor of justice studies in the School of Social Transformation at Arizona State University, USA. She is the author of *Battering States: The Politics of Domestic Violence in Israel* (Vanderbilt University Press, 2017), and coeditor (with Miriam Elman) of *Jerusalem: Conflict and Cooperation in a Contested State* (Syracuse University Press, 2014). She is a past president of the Association for Political and Legal Anthropology. Adelman co-founded GLSEN Phoenix in 2002 and is a current board member of the chapter; she is a founding member and former co-chair of GLSEN's National Advisory Council, chair of GLSEN's Research Ethics Review Committee, and a member of GLSEN's National Board of Directors and its Executive Committee.

Özlem Altıok, PhD, MPSA, is a principal lecturer in women's and gender studies, and international studies, at the University of North Texas, USA. Her teaching and research interests center on: the relationship between gender, politics, and religion; social policy; global political economy; immigration; and social movements. In addition to being a feminist teacher-scholar, Dr Altıok is also an active member of the Equality Watch Women's Group (EŞİTİZ) and Women's Platform for Equality (EŞİK) in Turkey.

Charity Anderson is a senior research associate at the Joseph C. Cornwall Center for Metropolitan Studies at Rutgers University-Newark, USA, and director of the Clemente Veterans' Initiative Newark, a humanities course for veterans and military-connected civilians. Her research interests include urban education, poverty and inequality, transformative learning, and humanities education for marginalized populations. She holds master's degrees in art history, education, and social work, and a PhD in social work from the University of Chicago.

Elinore Avni is a PhD student in the Sociology Department at Boston University, USA. She obtained her master's degree in sociology from Tel Aviv University. Her research interests include intergenerational relationships, aging and the life course, medical sociology, international sociology, and quantitative methodology.

Jason Brown is an associate professor in the School of Cultures, Languages & Linguistics at the University of Auckland, New Zealand. He has worked with endangered languages and indigenous communities throughout his career.

Kristen M. Budd, PhD, is an associate professor of sociology and criminology at Miami University in Oxford, Ohio, USA. She holds a PhD in sociology from Purdue University (2011), with a specialization in law and society. Her research focuses on interpersonal violence, law, and policy, including how they intersect with perpetrator and victim sociodemographic characteristics. Currently, she is researching patterns and predictors of offending behavior in relation to sexual assault, public perceptions in relation to criminal behavior, law, and criminal justice policy and practice, and social and legal responses to interpersonal violence and other social problems.

Eliza Byard earned a PhD in history at Columbia University. She is a leading global expert on LGBTQ+ issues in K-12 education and youth development. Under her leadership as deputy executive director (2001–08) and executive director (2008–21), GLSEN helped spur a significant decline in anti-LGBTQ+ violence in K-12 schools and established a professional norm of educator support for LGBTQ+ youth in the US. In 2009–10, she designed GLSEN's international research initiative in partnership with the United Nations Educational, Scientific, and Cultural Organization (UNESCO), providing new access to the United Nations (UN) and World Bank for LGBTQ+ education advocates. Byard has served as a trusted advisor to the Center for Disease Prevention and Control Division of Adolescent and School Health (CDC-DASH), the US Department of Education, the National Parks Service, Target, and Sodexo. She is currently on the boards of the Gill Foundation and CoQual, and the Board of Trustees of the America's Promise Alliance.

Carina Elisabeth Carlsen is a social worker and fat activist who lives in Oslo, Norway. She received her MA in empowerment and health promotion from the Department of Nursing and Health Promotion Work at OsloMet University.

Laurie Cooper Stoll is a professor of sociology at the University of Wisconsin-La Crosse, USA. She earned her PhD in sociology and graduate concentration in gender studies from Loyola University Chicago. She is the author of two books: *Race and Gender in the Classroom* (Lexington Books, 2013), winner of the 2015 Distinguished Contribution to Scholarship Book Award from the Race, Gender, and Class Section of the American Sociological Association; and *Should Schools Be Colorblind?* (Polity Books, 2019). She is the coeditor of the *Fat Studies* special issue "Standpoint Theory in Fat Studies" and has published several book chapters and articles in peer-reviewed journals. She is also the cocreator of the website www. twofatprofessors.com, which is committed to fighting fatphobia with education and community building.

John G. Dale is Associate Professor of Sociology and Director of Movement Engaged at George Mason University, USA. He has served as chair of the Global Division and the Transnational Initiatives Committee of the SSSP. He was recently a Japan Society for the Promotion of Science research fellow (2021–22) and a residential fellow at the Woodrow Wilson Center for International Scholars (2019–20). He currently serves on the Executive Steering Committee of the American Association for the Advancement of Science–Science and Human Rights Coalition and as a council member of the American Sociological Association's Section on Human Rights. He is author of *Free Burma: Transnational Legal Action and Corporate Accountability* (University of Minnesota Press, 2011) and co-author (with Anthony Orum) of *Political Sociology: Power and Participation in the Modern World* (Oxford University Press, 2008).

Héctor L. Delgado is Executive Officer of the SSSP and Professor Emeritus of Sociology, University of La Verne, USA. He is the author of *New Immigrants, Old Unions: Organizing Undocumented Workers in Los Angeles* (Temple University Press, 1993), one of the earliest and most influential books on the unionization of undocumented workers. Now retired, his research, publications, and teaching focused principally on immigrant workers, unionization, social class and inequality, race and ethnicity, and Latinx studies. Prior to obtaining his PhD at the University of Michigan in 1991, he worked in higher education student services for 20 years, recruiting and serving students of color.

Heather Dillaway is a professor of sociology at Wayne State University, USA. Previously, she completed a BA in sociology and history at Cornell University, an MA in sociology at the University of Delaware, and a PhD in sociology at Michigan State University. Her research focuses on women's menopause experiences and reproductive health experiences of women with physical disabilities. She participates in many editorial projects, including coediting an issue of *Gender & Society* on intersectionality and disability (in 2019), a book titled *Musings on Perimenopause and Menopause: Identity, Experience, and Transition* (Demeter Press, 2021), and volume 14 of *Research in Social Science and Disability* (Emerald, forthcoming).

Corey Dolgon teaches sociology at Stonehill College. He's written five books, including the award-winning *Kill It to Save It: An Autopsy of Capitalism's Triumph over Democracy* (Policy Press, 2017) and *The End of the Hamptons: Scenes from the Class Struggle in American Paradise* (NYU Press, 2005). He is a past-president of both the SSSP (2021) and the Association for Humanist Sociology (2008).

Stephen P. Gasteyer is an associate professor of sociology at Michigan State University, USA. His research focuses on community development, natural resources management, colonialism and resistance, and food and water justice, Recent research addresses comparative environmental equity in access to water and sanitation, including comparative work among communities in the US, Palestine, and a case study in Tanzania. He has previously worked as a tenure-stream professor at the University of Illinois (2005–08) and the Rural Community Assistance Partnership in Washington, DC (2002–05). He received a BA from Earlham College in 1987 and a PhD in sociology from Iowa State University in 2001.

Andrea N. Hunt is an associate professor of sociology and the founding director of the Mitchell-West Center for Social Inclusion at the University of North Alabama, USA. Her teaching, research, and community efforts cover a range of interrelated topics, including identity, inequality, and intersectional trauma-informed practices. Dr Hunt is a public sociologist and her current research focuses on the intersection of race, gender, and trauma in recovery narratives. She is currently pursuing a degree in clinical mental health counseling, with a specialization in addiction and career development to better support and advocate for her community.

Jerry A. Jacobs is a professor of sociology at the University of Pennsylvania, USA, where he teaches courses on social problems and the sociology of work. Jacobs served as editor of the *American Sociological Review* and was the founding president of the Work and Family Researchers Network. His recent research includes studies of ethnocentrism in sociology. He has authored six books, including *In Defense of Disciplines* (University of Chicago Press, 2013) and (with Kathleen Gerson) *The Time Divide: Work, Family and Gender Inequality* (Harvard University Press, 2004). His current project is a multifaceted exploration of the history and future of work that focuses on technology, gender, caring, and aging.

Ivan Kislenko is a PhD candidate at HSE University, Russia, and Ghent University, Belgium. Currently, he is a Fulbright visiting researcher at George Mason University, USA. Ivan has written his doctoral dissertation, "The idea of global sociology in the international sociological agenda: unity and diversity of interpretations," which is going to be defended in 2022. His research interests include global sociology, Southern theory, global knowledge production, and the history of sociological thought.

David C. Lane is an assistant professor in the Department of Criminal Justice Sciences at Illinois State University, USA. He holds a PhD in sociology from the University of Delaware. His monograph, *The Other End of the Needle: Continuity and Change among Tattoo Workers* (Rutgers University Press 2021) has recently been released. His research articles on tattoo work appear in *Deviant Behavior* and the *Sociology Compass*. He also serves as the chair of the Body Art and Images area of the Mid-Atlantic Popular and American Culture Association. Recently, his research expertise has been featured on *Inking of Immunity* podcast, Telemundo's *Radar 2021*, and Bloomberg's *Made*.

Seow Ting Lee is Professor of Strategic and Health Communication in the University of Colorado Boulder's Department of Advertising, Public Relations and Media Design, USA. Her research focuses on organization–stakeholder communication strategies and practices, with an emphasis on new media. Her research has been published in leading, peer-reviewed journals in the field, including the *Journal of Communication, Journal of Health Communication, Health Communication, Public Relations Review, Journal of Public Relations Research, Media, Culture and Society, Mass Communication and Society, Health Promotion International, Journal of Mass Media Ethics*, and *Place Branding and Public Diplomacy*.

Stephanie von Liebenstein is a writer, academic editor, and legal scholar in Berlin, Germany. She earned her MA in English, German, and philosophy, and studied law. She founded the German Association against Weight Discrimination (Gesellschaft gegen Gewichtsdiskriminierung e.V.) in 2005. She served as an editorial board member of *Fat Studies* from 2011 to 2014. In 2016, she served as an expert on weight discrimination at the Convention on the Evaluation of the General Equal Treatment Act 2006, hosted by the German federal antidiscrimination agency. She is the author of numerous publications, presentations, and appearances in the media, editor of the *Fat Studies* special issue "Fatness and Law," and host of the 2022 International Weight Stigma Conference in Berlin.

Angela Meadows is a lecturer in psychology at the University of Essex, UK. She is a social psychologist specializing in prejudice and discrimination relating to weight and body size. Her work focuses on how higher-weight people respond to the stigma they encounter in their daily lives, whether by internalizing their low status or by rejecting and challenging devaluation, and the implications both for individuals and for social change. She has published a number of articles and book chapters, and has been interviewed by numerous media outlets internationally. She writes on issues around weight and health for print and digital media. In 2013, she founded the Annual International Weight Stigma Conference, now in its eighth year.

John Middleton is a PhD candidate in linguistics at the University of Auckland, New Zealand, and a researcher with the Tokelauan language and community.

Glenn W. Muschert is a professor of sociology in the Department of Humanities and Social Sciences at Khalifa University of Science and Technology, Abu Dhabi, United Arab Emirates. His research focuses on digital society, sustainable development, and the ethical solution of social problems.

Ahmed Badawi Mustapha is a Research Fellow at the Institute of African Studies, University of Ghana, Ghana. His research focuses on Islam and Muslim societies (particularly in Africa), the interconnectedness of state and religion, militant organizations, political violence, radical ideologies, counterextremism, and broader socioeconomic issues concerning Africa. He has published articles and book chapters in this regard.

Manjusha Nair is an associate professor of sociology at George Mason University, USA. Before this, Dr Nair taught at the National University of Singapore. Dr Nair completed a PhD in sociology from Rutgers University and a master of philosophy in economics from Jawaharlal Nehru University in India. Dr Nair's research and teaching interests are in globalization, political sociology, comparative and historical sociology, development, labor movements, India, China, Ethiopia, and South Africa. Dr Nair's publications include an award-winning book, *Undervalued Dissent: Informal Workers' Politics in India* (SUNY Press, 2016), and articles in *Development and Change, Critical Sociology,* and *International Labor and Working-Class History*.

Marko Salvaggio is an environmental sociologist based in Mozambique and a faculty member in the School of Professional Advancement at Tulane University, USA. Prior to Tulane, he was an assistant professor of sociology and environmental studies at Goucher College. His areas of specialization include: environmental sociology; theories of nation, race, ethnicity, and indigeneity; cultural studies; and the political economy of space, place, and tourism. His current research aims at understanding climate change risk perceptions among coastal communities in southeastern Africa.

Marie Carmen Shingne, MSc, is a PhD candidate in the Michigan State University Sociology Department, USA, with specializations in animal studies, global urban studies, and community engaged research. She has studied multispecies urban access in India and water access in the US. She was a contributing researcher to the Closing the Water Access Gap Project conducted by DigDeep, the US Water Alliance, and Michigan State University sociologists. Her PhD dissertation project explores the importance of water as a nonhuman agent in political and infrastructural efforts to resolve water and sanitation access issues.

Jason A. Smith is a research affiliate faculty at the Center for Social Science Research at George Mason University, USA, and completed his PhD in sociology from the same institution in 2019. Dr Smith's research focuses on race and media exclusion, with overarching themes including issues related to access and representation for communities of color in various institutional and organizational spaces. Previous research has been published in *Ethnic & Racial Studies*, *Sociology of Race & Ethnicity*, and *Studies in Media and Communication*.

Noreen Sugrue is Director of Research at the Latino Policy Forum and SSSP President (2021–22). Before joining the forum, she was a faculty member at the University of Illinois at Urbana-Champaign. Through the lenses of inequity, inequality, and distributive justice, her research focus centers on issues related to immigration, immigrants, gender, healthcare, and workforce. In addition, she analyzes and evaluates the construction and implementation of social policies as means of both addressing and redressing inequities. Her work is published in both peer-reviewed and popular press venues; in addition, Sugrue has provided testimony to federal, state, and city legislative committees.

Catherine van de Ruit is an assistant professor at Ursinus College, USA. She earned her PhD in sociology at the University of Pennsylvania and undertook postdoctoral research at the Armstrong Institute for Patient Safety and Quality at Johns Hopkins University. Her research focuses on critical public health in Southern Africa and the US. She was awarded funding from the National Science Foundation (NSF) and South African National Research Foundation to study AIDS policy in South Africa, and she has a book manuscript in progress based on this research, titled *Outsourcing Obligation: The Organization of South African AIDS Care*.

Amy Zhou is an Assistant Professor in the Department of Sociology at Barnard College, USA. She earned her PhD in sociology at the University of California Los Angeles and undertook postdoctoral research at the Institute for Practical Ethics at the University of California San Diego. Her research and teaching interests are in the areas of medical sociology, inequality, development, race/ethnicity, and science and technology studies. Her work broadly explores how social conditions and institutions come to bear on healthcare practices and experiences of health and illness.

Acknowledgments

This volume would not have been possible without the cooperation and support of so many good people. We, the editors, wish to thank our authors first, both for working with us and for their quality contributions. It is a pleasure to work with such a group of professionals to bring ideas to print. As always, we are indebted to Michele Koontz and Héctor Delgado of the SSSP administrative and executive offices, respectively, for their support and encouragement. We thank acquisitions editor Victoria Pittman and her team at Policy Press, with whom we are pleased to collaborate. Finally, we thank all our fellow students, scholars, and activists, who make the SSSP such an exciting environment in which to study, research, write, and undertake meaningful social action.

Foreword

Margaret Abraham

Social justice is arguably one of the key guiding principles that should inform human social exchange. Social justice draws our attention to embedded issues of wealth, resource distribution, oppression, representation, recognition, and access. It is a key component in identifying and addressing changes needed across the globe. Today, in a violent, unequal, and divided world, striving for social justice seems a challenging endeavor. The most astounding achievements in science and technology, in medicine, and in the arts have created a world that has the potential to provide every human being with a life of equality, dignity, security, and well-being. Yet, the reality is that inequalities and injustices persist, taking new forms and growing. While there is some progress for social justice, this progress is uneven.

Addressing social justice is not new terrain for the social sciences. However, there is an increasing urgency in studying/theorizing/researching, as well as linking knowledge and practice, in these challenging times. The onset of the COVID-19 global pandemic and the responses to this pandemic have amplified entrenched inequalities and vulnerabilities, and exposed the fatal flaws in our social, political, and economic structures. In addition to the immense tragic loss of millions of lives, the pandemic has disproportionately impacted the lives, livelihoods, and well-being of large numbers of people, especially the most disadvantaged. It has increased wealth disparities, created immense uncertainty for many, and exacerbated fear and hardships, including food insecurity, unemployment and underemployment, violence, disruptions and challenges in education, digital divides, crises in care, mental health vulnerabilities, and problems of migration, displacement, and statelessness. What is promising, however, is the forms of resistance and resilience by individuals, communities, and movements across the globe, connecting and collaborating to challenge systemic injustices, and striving for social justice and social change.

Given the state of our world, a global agenda for social justice includes addressing the violence, discrimination, and exclusions that pervade societies worldwide. The persistence, prevalence, and pervasiveness of gender-based and intersectional violence require continued attention at the micro, meso, and macro levels. The increased numbers of displaced people with little or no option due to migration barriers is a humanitarian crisis that requires immediate global attention. Addressing growing economic disparities, poverty, climate change, unfettered capitalism, diminishing democracies, and rising authoritarianism is crucial. Equally important is to address unequal education, the lack of such fundamental rights as access to water, freedom of expression, affordable housing, and healthcare (including global access to vaccines and mental healthcare), and the lack of safe working conditions and labor rights in the informal and formal sectors.

Over several decades, the SSSP has played a pivotal role in highlighting social concerns and has emphasized the importance of linking rigorous research and practice. The editors and authors of this volume further compel us to consider some key issues in a global agenda for social justice. Drawing on a contextual global sociology and using a spectrum of methodologies to conceptualize and connect, they highlight major social problems and offer possible pathways for social change. They show that sociological analysis, engagement, and intervention is necessary, and that this is a time to (re) imagine and work together to build an equal, just, peaceful, and sustainable world for all.

PART I

Topical pieces

ONE

The challenge of global school segregation

Charity Anderson

The problem

School segregation—the uneven distribution of students across schools, based on their socioeconomic status (SES), sex, race/ethnicity, or other ascribed characteristics—has important implications for educational inequality, social cohesion, and intergenerational mobility (Bonal and Bellei, 2019). While this topic has drawn special attention in the US, due, in part, to the 1954 *Brown v. the Board of Education* Supreme Court case, between-school segregation is a concern to policymakers and researchers worldwide. School segregation by race dominates much of the research on this topic in the US, but studies of school segregation by SES predominate internationally. This chapter summarizes what we know about between-school segregation by SES, describing the strongest international evidence we have, drawing attention to the consequences of segregation and the benefits of integration, and concluding with a discussion of solutions.

Residential segregation, migration movements, economic inequalities, and even education policies themselves have shaped a growing process of school segregation between the world's most disadvantaged students and the wealthiest. School composition matters, and it impacts students' short- and long-term academic and social-emotional outcomes. Student performance is more strongly related to SES than to other school compositional characteristics, such as gender, immigrant status, or race/ethnicity. Indeed, research indicates that disadvantaged students who attend schools with more affluent peers see a range of positive effects, including increased achievement, motivation, and resiliency (Van Ewijk and Sleegers, 2010; Agasisti et al, 2021). A school's average SES is highly predictive of its academic climate and instructional quality, both factors associated with educational outcomes. School segregation is negatively associated with the achievement of the most economically disadvantaged students and has been shown to affect school attendance, grade retention, and student behavior (Palardy, 2013; Palardy et al, 2015).

Clustering low-SES students together exacerbates inequality. Isolating students deprives them of opportunities to learn, interact, and communicate with youth from different backgrounds, and prevents them from developing broad social networks. Segregated schools thus inadequately prepare students for the diverse world they will enter post-graduation, which, in turn, threatens social mobility and cohesion.

Research evidence

Segregation is a complex concept that cannot be wholly captured by a single indicator. A common way of analyzing school segregation is to measure the extent to which students are evenly (or unevenly) distributed across schools. Studies of international school segregation often focus on Organisation for Economic Cooperation and Development (OECD) member countries and draw on data gathered from the Programme for International Student Assessment (PISA)—a triennial, large-scale international assessment that has been administered since 2000.

PISA data gathered over 15 years (2000–15) indicate that Nordic countries (with the exception of Denmark), Iceland, Scotland, and Wales have the most socially integrated schools (Gutiérrez et al, 2020). In Finland, Norway, and Sweden, for example, less than 43 per cent of disadvantaged students (students whose value on the PISA index of economic, social, and cultural status [ESCS] is among the bottom 25 per cent of students within their country or economy) attend disadvantaged schools (schools in the bottom 25 per cent of the national distribution of the school-level ESCS index). Conversely, Chile, Hungary, and Mexico have exceptionally segregated schools. This finding is consistent with previous international research which found countries that "track" students at an early age (for example, Austria, Belgium, Germany, and Hungary) also tend to be more socially segregated (Jenkins et al, 2008). Tracking is the practice of separating students into groups based on their perceived ability or academic achievement. In Hungary and Mexico, as well as nine additional OECD countries—Australia, Belgium, Chile, the Czech Republic, France, Israel, the Slovak Republic, Spain, and the US—over half of all disadvantaged students attend disadvantaged schools (OECD, 2018). Across OECD countries, less than 7 per cent of disadvantaged students attend advantaged schools (schools in the top 25 per cent of the national distribution of the school-level ESCS index) (OECD, 2018).

When socioeconomic segregation between schools is high, disadvantaged students are more at risk of being "left behind" in schools with high concentrations of low achievers. When students from low-SES families attend schools of concentrated disadvantage, they are more likely to perform poorly. PISA data consistently demonstrate that both student SES and school socioeconomic profile (that is, the average SES of students in a school) are strongly associated with student achievement. Students who come from more advantaged backgrounds, and whose peers are also more advantaged, score higher on the PISA. Disadvantaged students attending disadvantaged schools are therefore doubly disadvantaged.

School systems across the world have seen, at best, only marginal changes in between-school segregation over time. Only Poland has shown important declines in segregation since 2000. Overall, the amount of between-school variation in most countries did not change between 2000 and 2015, which is a staggering finding given the significant economic and political events during those 15 years—for example, increased migration due to conflict and climate change, the Global Recession of 2007–09, rising income and wealth inequality, and worldwide education reforms, including increased access to schooling. Segregation of the wealthiest and poorest 20 per cent of students from other groups remains pronounced, and the pattern is particularly evident in countries with high levels of segregation (Gutiérrez et al, 2020). This leads to an important conclusion: between-school segregation is, to a great degree, structurally entrenched; that is, patterns of student sorting have become embedded in institutions and institutionalized thinking over time, and have grown highly resistant to change.

Several factors may explain the persistence of between-school segregation. When assignment to schools is mainly based on a family's residence, as is the case in most OECD countries, segregation at school typically reproduces neighborhood segregation. School policies, such as tracking, also contribute to stratification, as advantaged students are often overrepresented in academic tracks while disadvantaged students are more frequently relegated to vocational tracks. School choice policies may also play a role. Empirical evidence from Chile, New Zealand, Sweden, the UK, and the US suggests that school choice "reforms" tend to increase segregation because more affluent, educated families are more likely to make better-informed choices, thus concentrating advantaged students in the "best" schools (OECD, 2018). Segregation is further intensified when schools select students based on academic and/or financial criteria (for example, through school fees). Evidence from Chile, for example, suggests that the rise in private schools funded through vouchers has led to an increase in socioeconomic segregation in schools because advantaged parents are more likely than disadvantaged parents to choose private schools for their children.

Recommendations and solutions

Around the world, public policies directly aimed at reducing school segregation by SES are largely absent. In most countries, school segregation has not been identified as a matter of policy, and governments have been disinclined to introduce significant changes to achieve a more balanced distribution of students across schools. Research indicates that structural factors are the probable drivers of between-school segregation, and some of the factors contributing to school segregation are external to education systems—like residential segregation—and require action beyond education policy.

School segregation is deeply contextual, and policies to address segregation should differ across the world. The same desegregation measures used in one context could induce segregation, or have a null effect, in other contexts. For example, the Education Reform Act of 1988, which extended school choice in the UK, did not impact school segregation, while the voucher system in Chile significantly increased school segregation. Similarly, school district mapping or zoning (that is, policies that regulate the flow of students among schools, often assigning pupils to schools based on residence) has mitigated school segregation in some areas of Spain but has proven largely ineffective in France (Bonal and Bellei, 2019). The contextual nature of school segregation explains the absence of universal solutions.

Despite the challenges in addressing between-school segregation around the world, achieving equity in schools is a social justice imperative. PISA data show that one of the most important factors affecting a student's performance is the socioeconomic background of the other students in the school. This implies that one of the most critical resources to be allocated to schools is the students themselves. To mitigate school segregation, policymakers might generally consider the following areas.

Residential segregation

Addressing residential segregation is necessary to reduce school segregation. Many schools with large proportions of low-SES students are segregated because they are located in segregated neighborhoods. The degree of social diversity in schools depends on how students are allocated across schools. In almost all school systems, students are assigned to public schools based on their home address. Students are typically assigned to the school closest to their residence, often to avoid long commutes. Geographic assignment may have the unintended consequence of reproducing, and even reinforcing, patterns of residential segregation. However, the relationship between residential segregation and school segregation is complex and nonlinear. Residential segregation impacts school segregation as much as differences in school quality impact families' residential choices and decisions, especially among more affluent families.

Neighborhood homogeneity, areas of concentrated poverty, and demographic trends are potential factors that contribute to school segregation and cannot be addressed through education policy alone. Mitigation requires developing urban development policies, social policies, or cultural actions to encourage social integration. In addition to antidiscrimination laws, which outlaw discrimination in housing, policy options might include:

- scatter-site programs (for example, distributing public housing across a range of neighborhoods);
- rental subsidies and housing vouchers (for example, allowing residents to choose housing and receive a subsidy to cover rent);
- housing diversification (for example, replacing old housing stock with homes that vary in size, form, price, and so on to attract both owners and renters);
- housing allocation procedures (for example, engineering the composition of certain neighborhoods to reduce concentrations of high- or low-income residents); and
- social integration policies, particularly for low-SES immigrants (for example, providing access to local jobs and education, citizenship acquisition, and basic services) (Iceland, 2014).

In the US, policies to reduce residential segregation have focused more on giving individuals flexibility and mobility in their housing choices, while Europe has focused more on city and neighborhood planning. To date, no single policy has proven to be completely effective in reducing residential segregation, but each has been associated with modest results.

School choice

In the last 25 years, more than two thirds of OECD countries have increased the extent of parental school choice in public and, in some countries, private schools. Parents' "preferences," however, can result in segregating students by ability, SES, and race/ethnicity. For example, research shows that more affluent parents tend to avoid schools with large numbers of disadvantaged students. Providing choice to parents should be done without exacerbating segregation and inequity. This can be achieved by introducing specific criteria to the allocation of students across schools—often called "controlled choice." Controlled choice, which partially diminishes parents' freedom to choose a school for their child, is present in some cities of the Netherlands, the US, and Spain. Different systems of controlled choice can be used to ensure a balanced distribution of pupils, including:

- reserving a set number or proportion of seats in schools for students from different socioeconomic backgrounds;
- using lotteries or formulae to assign seats in schools; and
- centralizing procedures to match students to schools, for example, relying on a clearly defined set of criteria that includes SES (engaging schools and

communities in outlining these criteria can ensure that they are sensitive to local contexts and can help ease implementation).

Controlled choice systems are complex, require centralized administration, and give local authorities some degree of control over schools' admissions procedures. Allocation mechanisms vary across countries, and their effectiveness depends on the school system's capacity to match parents' preference for high-quality schools with a consistent application of criteria benefiting disadvantaged students. Such policies support those who typically exercise choice the least and limit schools' ability to "cherry-pick" students, thus balancing market mechanisms with a more equitable distribution of students across schools.

Selection

School choice exists in most countries, but parents' ability to exercise that choice is constrained by factors like selective admissions, which can be a source of inequality and stratification within school systems. Research demonstrates that "reforms" that provide schools with high levels of discretion in student admissions—including aptitude tests, interviews, and other school entrance requirements—increase inequity. Admission practices often lack transparency and are prone to unpredictability. To address the role of admissions in school segregation, policymakers might:

- empower an independent body to establish admissions criteria—this prevents schools from selecting students based on criteria that benefit some students over others; and
- set and adhere to a systemwide registration time—this levels the playing field and does not privilege better-informed parents, who tend to enroll their children in the school of their choice early on.

Tracking

Once students are admitted, they are often subject to academic selection, or tracking. Selection occurs in all OECD countries, but some countries, such as Austria and Germany, begin tracking when students are just ten years old. Students from low-SES backgrounds are adversely affected by academic selection, and especially by early tracking. They are disproportionally placed in the least academically oriented tracks early on, which amplifies inequities. Lower tracks tend to receive fewer human and material resources, and they are often avoided by the strongest teachers. Student trajectories are marked by their assignment to lower tracks, with little opportunity to move to higher tracks. Policymakers focused on equity and school desegregation might:

- eliminate tracking altogether or delay it until a student is in upper-secondary education;
- limit the number of subjects and/or duration of tracking;
- offer opportunities to change tracks; and
- maintain high curricular and instructional standards for all tracks.

While elimination of tracking is often seen as a key part of desegregation policies, defenders of the practice argue that it is a way to maintain a degree of social heterogeneity within public schools. Although there is abundant evidence that tracking limits learning for *all* students, middle- and upper-class families often advocate for tracking, believing that it generates opportunities for their children (Mickelson and Nkomo, 2012). Tracking is a trade-off, then. Without it, affluent families would likely migrate to private schools, further exacerbating class segregation.

Incentives

Incentives are another method to potentially mitigate school segregation. Incentives may be directed toward schools and/or families:

- Financial incentives can be provided to schools for selecting low-SES students, for example, by weighting the funds received by the schools. Various governments have implemented compensatory financing mechanisms. Chile, Belgium, and the Netherlands have introduced weighted funding, where money follows the student on a per-pupil basis and the amount provided depends on the SES and education needs of each student. These incentives are designed to target disadvantaged students and, in doing so, make low-SES students more attractive to schools competing for enrollment (Schleicher, 2018). This may partially explain why disadvantaged students in the Netherlands are relatively less segregated into certain schools.
- Vouchers, or tuition certificates, can be provided to low-SES families to use to enroll students in "approved" schools. Targeting vouchers specifically to disadvantaged families, rather than offering them to all families, prevents schools from "skimming" wealthier students. It is important to note, though, that even where vouchers reduce the cost of private schools, "hidden" fees—for extracurricular activities, uniforms, trips, and so on—can still make them unaffordable in practice. To detractors, voucher programs divert public resources to private entities, consequently depriving public schools, which tend to serve large populations of disadvantaged students, of the resources they need to provide high-quality education for all students.

References

Agasisti, T., Avvisati, F., Borgonovi, F., and Longobardi, S. (2021) What school factors are associated with the success of socio-economically disadvantaged students? An empirical investigation using PISA data. *Social Indicators Research*, 157: 749–81. Available at: https://doi.org/10.1007/s11205-021-02668-w

Bonal, X. and Bellei, C. (eds) (2019) *Understanding School Segregation. Patterns, Causes and Consequences of Spatial Inequalities in Education.* London: Bloomsbury.

Gutiérrez, G., Jerrim, J., and Torres, R. (2020) School segregation across the world: has any progress been made in reducing the separation of the rich from the poor? *The Journal of Economic Inequality*, 18: 157–79. Available at: https://doi.org/10.1007/s10888-019-09437-3

Iceland, J. (2014) Residential segregation: a transatlantic analysis. Available at: www.migrationpolicy.org/sites/default/files/publications/TCM_Cities_Residential-SegregationFINALWEB.pdf

Jenkins, S., Micklewright, J., and Schnepf, S. (2008) Social segregation in secondary schools: how does England compare with other countries? *Oxford Review of Education*, 34(1): 21–37. Available at: https://doi.org/10.1080/03054980701542039

Mickelson, R.A. and Nkomo, M. (2012) Integrated schooling, life course outcomes, and social cohesion in multiethnic democratic societies. *Review of Research in Education*, 36: 197–238. Available at: https://doi.org/10.3102/0091732X11422667

OECD (Organisation for Economic Cooperation and Development) (2018) Equity in education: breaking down barriers to social mobility. Paris: OECD Publishing. Available at: https://doi.org/10.1787/9789264073234-en

Palardy, G.J. (2013) High school socioeconomic segregation and student attainment. *American Educational Research Journal*, 50(4): 714–54. Available at: https://doi.org/10.3102/0002831213481240

Palardy, G.J., Rumberger, R.W., and Butler, T. (2015) The effect of high school socioeconomic, racial, and linguistic segregation on academic performance and school behaviors. *Teachers College Record*, 117(12): 1–53.

Schleicher, A. (2018) *World Class: How to Build a 21st Century School System.* Paris: OECD Publishing. Available at: https://doi.org/10.1787/9789264300002-4-en

Van Ewijk, R. and Sleegers, P. (2010) The effect of peer socioeconomic status on student achievement: a meta-analysis. *Educational Research Review*, 5(2): 134–50. Available at: https://doi.org/10.2139/ssrn.1402645

Further reading

Benito, R., Alegre, M.À., and Gonzàlez-Balletbò, I. (2014) School segregation and its effects on educational equality and efficiency in 16 OECD comprehensive school systems. *Comparative Education Review*, 58(1): 104–34. Available at: www.jstor.org/stable/10.1086/672011

Boterman, W., Musterd, S., Pacchi, C., and Ranci, C. (eds) (2019) Special issue: school segregation in contemporary cities: socio-spatial dynamics and urban outcomes. *Urban Studies*, 56(15).

Cordini, M. (2019) School segregation: institutional rules, spatial constraints and households' agency. *International Review of Sociology*, 29(2): 279–96. Available at: https://doi.org/10.1080/03906701.2019.1641276

OECD (Organisation for Economic Cooperation and Development) (2019) *Balancing School Choice and Equity: An International Perspective Based on PISA*. Paris: OECD Publishing. Available at: https://doi.org/10.1787/2592c974-en

The authoritarian backlash against education justice for lesbian, gay, bisexual, transgender, and queer youth

Madelaine Adelman and Eliza Byard

The problem

The global fight against the victimization of lesbian, gay, bisexual, transgender, and queer (LGBTQ+) youth has led to a prolific backlash. The LGBTQ+ "safe schools" movement has gotten violence based on sexual orientation and gender identity recognized as a problem by the United Nations (UN). However, this victory has resulted in the greater availability of anti-LGBTQ+ tropes for use as political fodder by bad-faith actors seeking to undermine progress toward the rights of LGBTQ+ youth, in particular, and democratic values, more generally. We are specifically concerned in this chapter with how opportunistic anti-LGBTQ+ state regimes clash with the UN vision for LGBTQ+-inclusive sustainable development, with resulting harm to LGBTQ+ youth. In this first section, we describe the safe schools movement, explain its connection to the UN's commitment to education justice, and point to how countermovements around the globe endeavor to quash the hard-won achievements of LGBTQ+ rights movements by targeting sexual and gender minority youth.

Following the lead of sexual and gender minority youth who have begun to demand safety and dignity around the world, the global safe schools movement is an informal network of nongovernmental organizations (NGOs) active on nearly every continent. It is concerned with the prevalence and effects of bias-based violence and discrimination against primary and secondary school students who do not conform to socially dominant or expected sexuality and gender norms. The transnational movement is united by two shared goals: to document LGBTQ+ youth experiences through research; and to promote affirming school climates through advocacy. Ultimately, this combination of research and advocacy has led intergovernmental organizations, such as the UN, to encourage states to acknowledge and protect LGBTQ+ youth.

Notably, the UN (2015a) argues that LGBTQ+ safety and equality is central to its Agenda 2030 plan for achieving global peace and prosperity, particularly in terms of Goals 3 (Good Health and Well-being), 4 (Quality Education), and 5 (Gender Equality). To that end, in 2015, several UN agencies declared that advancing the UN's Sustainable Development Goals (SDGs) would be unreachable if states failed to protect LGBTQ+ individuals, as well as those perceived as LGBTQ+, and their families, against violence and discriminatory laws and practices, including within the education sector (UN, 2015b). Education, they argued, is a basic human right that delivers lifelong benefits to individuals, families, and the state, including emotional well-being and economic security.

The emergence of new norms to protect LGBTQ+ youth has sparked a backlash strongly associated with right-wing authoritarian regimes. As sociologist Beth Hess (1999) argues, such efforts do not happen in the dark. Indeed, intentional attacks on those at the margins often occur during periods of social and economic instability. Whether values-driven or more cynically strategic to mobilize supporters, right-wing parties—often in tandem with evangelical and other fundamentalist religious groups—encourage actions against LGBTQ+ youth in the name of their protection. Such countermovements: deny equal access to education to a marginalized population; undo years of work to promote greater health, well-being, and belonging among LGBTQ+ youth; and, gamble with a state's ability to deliver on the UN Agenda 2030's SDGs.

Research evidence

The Pew Research Center (2020) finds that global levels of acceptance of "homosexuality" vary by age, education, religiosity, political ideology, and a state's per capita gross domestic product. According to the Williams Institute's Global Acceptance Index (GAI), between 1981 and 2020, 56 of 175 countries and locations have observed increases in acceptance of LGBTQ+ people, 57 have observed decreases, and 62 have observed no measurable change (Flores, 2019). Notably, the GAI indicates that the divergence in attitude has become more polarized in recent years, with the gap expanding between the most and least accepting countries. Although it is difficult to determine the direction of a causal relationships among public attitudes, policy changes, and political campaigns, we can say with confidence that right-wing elites are hijacking anti-LGBTQ+ animus to attract support for their authoritarian aims.

Over the last decade, right-wing countermovements have coalesced around an antidemocratic worldview. Political scientist Leigh Payne and anthropologist Andreza Aruska de Souza Santos (2020) find that this worldview relies on fear, threat, and nostalgia, framed by conservatism and morality, whereby a state's resources—including protections and responsibilities associated with individual rights—are allocated to those who can demonstrate their public worth. Political scientist Michael Bosia (2013) argues that common frames and tactics used to demonize LGBTQ+ people— by defining them as existential threats to the nation-state—circulate and reinforce each other in places as disparate as Latin America, Eastern Europe, and North America. Political scientist José Manuel Morán Faúndes (2019) examines how similar vows to combat "gender ideology"[1] and "cultural Marxism,"[2] offered in the name of "defending the family" and "protecting the children," are used to target feminists and LGBTQ+ people, and to undo progress on LGBTQ+-inclusive education.

A right-wing group induced a moral panic against LGBTQ+ and feminist movements in Brazil, for example, uniting its followers in defense of the traditional family. Bolsonaro's presidential campaign in the country co-opted this trope and won in 2019. Upon taking office, he set out to eliminate all references to LGBTQ+ topics, as well as feminism and violence against women, in Brazilian schools. In Russia, political scientist Fernando Nuñez-Mietz (2019) analyzes how a parallel phenomenon has emerged since the fall of the Soviet Union, where an alliance emerged between the Russian Orthodox Church, which has fostered the notion that "nontraditional" sexual orientations and gender identities (SOGI) are to blame for Russia's moral crisis, and Putin's regime, which has enacted legislation to guard against the so-called "recruitment of children" into "nontraditional" SOGI. In the US, following their failure to halt marriage equality, right-wing groups, such as Alliance Defending Freedom, have sought the legal erasure of trans youth. State legislators want transgender youth to participate in physical education and sport based on their "sex assigned at birth" rather than their gender identity, while also barring trans youth from obtaining gender-affirming healthcare. Endorsed by Trump through his federal Departments of Justice and Education, these anti-trans debates and policies have caused deep health and education disparities among US youth.

Antidemocratic antagonism targeting LGBTQ+ youth has multiplied exponentially in the last decade, resulting in violence and legalized discrimination. A central part of right-wing electoral campaigns and subsequent political regimes is the branding of LGBTQ+ people as second-class citizens, if not disloyal outsiders. This troubling backlash harms LGBTQ+ youth and undermines a state's aspirations to meet the shared global priorities reflected in the UN Agenda 2030's SDGs.

The effort to measure LGBTQ+ perspectives on youth and education is a relatively new area of research. Stigma and lack of capacity have constrained investment in it by scholars, funders, government agencies, and advocacy groups. Data on SOGI are not typically collected in research. In the US, SOGI are newly added yet still optional state-based questions in the Centers for Disease Control and Prevention's (CDC's) Youth Risk Behavior Survey (see www.cdc.gov/yrbs). LGBTQ+ youth are also not an easily accessible population, and parental consent may be difficult, if not dangerous, due to family rejection.

Today, we observe a rising trajectory of research regarding LGBTQ+ perspectives on schooling. GLSEN,[3] a US education organization focused on LGBTQ+ inclusion in K-12 schools, as well as their research partners in other countries, conduct national school climate surveys based on student self-reports, producing a growing baseline of evidence about the high prevalence of violence and discrimination against sexual and gender minority youth (Kosciw and Pizmony-Levy, 2016; Kosciw and Zongrone, 2019). Researchers also have generated local and regional analyses of student (and teacher) experiences. The United Nations Educational, Scientific, and Cultural Organization's (UNESCO) 2016 study of homophobic and transphobic violence around the world found pervasive bias in schools, ranging from expressions of anti-LGBTQ+ prejudice, to severe, institutionalized violence and discrimination. The UN now describes the overarching phenomenon of school-related gender-based violence (SRGBV) as a global crisis (UNESCO/UNGEI, 2016).

Research also examines how anti-LGBTQ+ violence and discrimination undermine youth development and educational attainment in ways similar to how systemic bias directed at other dimensions of youth identity (for example, sexism, racism, xenophobia, or ableism) produces health, education, and economic disparities. UNESCO (2016), GLSEN, and other researchers (Kosciw and Pizmony-Levy, 2016) find that students immersed in a hostile learning environment experience lower levels of school belonging, poorer educational outcomes, and other pernicious effects of minority stress on their health and economic welfare. According to the World Bank (2015), this lack of education justice, when bundled with a lack of employment and housing justice, means that LGBTQ+ people are likely overrepresented among the "bottom 40 per cent." In this way, a state's health and prosperity can be measured or predicted by how well the government treats its LGBTQ+ youth.

Research agenda framing to produce youth-centered knowledge

Research will be a critical step required to address the manifestations and manipulations of emerging core divisions organized around anti-LGBTQ+ tropes. Researchers and advocates will together want to ask questions about authoritarian backlash efforts targeting LGBTQ+ youth, such as:

- From where have these anti-LGBTQ+ tropes been exported? And along which routes have they been imported?
- Why do similar tropes develop and gain traction in disparate contexts?
- To what extent are anti-LGBTQ+ tropes incorporated in uneven ways in any one particular context?
- How do these tropes affect all community members, regardless of actual or perceived sexual orientation and gender identity or expression?
- What other kinds of inequalities and discrimination are tied into the dynamic of scapegoating against sexual and gender minority youth? Why, when, and where are refugees or immigrants, Jews, LGBTQ+ people, Muslims, or others blamed for social ills?
- Who benefits from the circulation, escalation, and institutionalization of these tropes?

At the same time, when discussing such questions as these, we recommend avoiding the very kind of binary and uncritical thinking that has constrained the lives of LGBTQ+ people, for example:

- sexual orientation and gender identity are neither static nor universal categories of identity;
- there are not wholly "good states" and "bad states";
- the notion of human rights comes with its own historical and cultural baggage; and
- measuring compliance with UN instruments is a neither fully transparent nor satisfactory process.

A range of case-study, comparative, and longitudinal research is needed to document and explain the trend of generating animus against LGBTQ+ youth to mobilize support for authoritarian regimes.

In the face of backlash against LGBTQ+ youth promulgated in the name of "protecting children," stakeholders of all ages and at all levels—local school communities, civil society actors, national governments, and multilateral organizations—have roles to play in defending and extending progress on state and global goals for youth development and education. In many ways, the solutions mirror the efforts necessary for the advancement of students facing discrimination due to other characteristics, such as sex, race, ethnicity, ability, national origin, and religion.

However, the pervasive and violent nature of anti-LGBTQ+ animus and its history of deployment as a weapon to exacerbate existing political and religious polarizations at the national and multilateral levels greatly complicate efforts to mobilize collectively for necessary action. Around the world, in Barbados, China, South Korea, sub-Saharan Africa, and the US, to name just a few regions, LGBTQ+ people—and the human rights mechanisms developed to acknowledge and protect them—have been framed as existential threats to kin and country, as anathema to national independence and moral purity, and as sources of economic inequality and political instability.

In short, two moves must be made simultaneously. The social problem of anti-LGBTQ+ bias in schools still needs to be addressed, while the backlash aimed at restoring the status quo ante needs to be unpacked and de-weaponized. Demonizing one group of people (any group) reveals the vulnerability of democratic institutions, such that mutually reinforcing efforts are required to prop them up. Identity-based movements are critical but insufficient without attention to the other SDGs outlined in the UN Agenda 2030, and vice versa. In other words, fighting for LGBTQ+ rights in schools can address environmental justice and sustainability concerns, along with poverty and economic inequality, while fighting for sustainable development can address LGBTQ+ rights in schools; however, the relationships must be articulated explicitly and be set in motion to work in concert with each other by researchers and advocates alike.

Perhaps the most important counterbalance to these entrenched disadvantages is the growing self-actualization, visibility, and advocacy of LGBTQ+ youth themselves in many countries. The International Lesbian, Gay, Bisexual, Transgender, Queer & Intersex Youth and Student Organization (ILGYO), for example, is a network of over 40 youth development organizations, from the UK to Turkey, who prepare LGBTQI youth to lead within LGBTQI and human rights sectors, and, in doing so, create a network of youth activists. In turn, this guarantees that state and international officials and decisionmakers will have to engage with and listen to LGBTQ+ youth.

Youth are now part of transnational advocacy in the room where it happens. For example, the UN 2020 Class of Young Leaders for the SDGs includes Bulgarian activist Martin Karadzhov, Chair of The International Lesbian, Gay, Bisexual, Trans and Intersex Association's (ILGA) World's Youth Steering Committee, a global LGBTQ+ NGO. Together, these young leaders mobilize youth around the world to advocate for SDGs. In the US, youth stand on the front lines of trans activism by sharing their stories on social media and testifying in state legislatures, despite the harmful responses they receive, both from online trolls and elected officials.

Youth voices in movement advocacy can continue to be amplified by parents, teachers, NGO staff, social service agency workers, and business leaders calling for systems change in education policies and practices. This will require the growth and maturation of civil society organizations focused on the safety and needs of their local LGBTQ+ communities. LGBTQ+ and other NGOs alike also will need to:

- unlearn ageism and adultism (along with racism, ableism, and so on);
- add youth to the table as present rather than future leaders;
- create room for youth liberation and youth power; and
- establish intergenerational models of leadership and social movements.

In addition to their advocacy, youth are also critical to the production of knowledge about school climate. The surge in research documenting their experiences in schools across North and South America, East Asia, the Middle East, Eastern and Western Europe, Africa, and the Pacific, for example, would be impossible without their participation. These studies have provided the data required to raise public awareness, catalyze grassroots groups, and influence decisionmakers to ameliorate education opportunities for LGBTQ+ students.

The fact that LGBTQ+ people and those who stand in solidarity with them are represented in all communities—national, ethnic, migrant, disabled, and religious—provides the potential for leadership and engagement that is rooted locally in all sectors of the globe, with the acknowledgment that each context presents a unique combination of safety and danger. Another important point of leverage for these efforts is the history of global focus on the needs of other marginalized groups of children, particularly gender-based violence and discrimination targeting women and girls. Collaboration via networks, partnerships, and coalitions across children's and education advocacy sectors will multiply their respective impact potential and lead to cross-sector learning and unanticipated insights.

Solutions

Finally, in this section, we conclude by outlining how to interrupt the backlash by creating healthy learning environments for LGBTQ+ students. Research suggests that systems change efforts at all levels will help to ensure the safety, education, and health of LGBTQ+ students. Some recommendations are aimed more narrowly at the school community, while others focus on society as a whole. Underlying all proposed solutions is the need for investment in and a valuing of SOGI data to: document the extent of the problem; identify variations of need and experience within and across populations; assess existing and possible solutions; and deliver reliable and translatable evidence to measure against established SDGs. Ameliorating the data gap can be pursued by:

- normalizing research on SOGI, including studies that make explicit the heteronormative and/or cisgender background of participants;
- incorporating SOGI identities in youth and education research;

- asking SOGI-related questions by using recommended practices in large-scale surveys;
- conducting qualitative research on SOGI perspectives;
- acknowledging the intersectionality of LGBTQ+ youth; and,
- focusing research on multiple dimensions of LGBTQ+ life.

Over time, enhancing our evidence base will also contribute to future knowledge exchanges and make cross-country analyses possible. Doing so will enable the development of human capital and access to social and economic justice for all through "data advocacy."

The following steps at the local, national, and multilateral levels will help preserve progress made to date and lay the foundation for further advancement of the well-being and educational opportunity of youth around the globe:

- Local efforts:
  - explore what it means to be an ally and stand in solidarity with LGBTQ+ youth;
  - listen to students to find out their priorities and needs;
  - vote your values;
  - get engaged in school-board elections;
  - attend school governance meetings;
  - examine policies and practices in your local school community that directly and indirectly inform the quality of life of LGBTQ+ students (for example, nondiscrimination policies, antiharassment policies, trans-inclusion policies, discriminatory application of facially neutral policies, and so on);
  - reform existing policies and institute new evidence-based policies and practices regarding supportive educators, inclusive curriculum, school–family partnerships, and other education access and equity initiatives;
  - talk with community members and hold elected officials accountable about shared concerns regarding school discipline, funding, inclusive curriculum, and diverse education staff; and,
  - explore what pursuing UN Agenda 2030 looks like to you and your school community, especially Target 4 ('Ensure inclusive and quality education for all and promote lifelong learning').
- National-level efforts:
  - raise awareness about the existence, needs, and strengths of LGBTQ+ youth who come from all walks of life;
  - conduct school climate research to document evidence of the extent of the violence and the efficacy of solutions;
  - integrate data about LGBTQ+ perspectives on education into public conversations about a healthy economy (for example, Estonians are

concerned about brain drain, so ask about the postgraduation plans of all youth);

- advocate for statewide legal protections that do not contribute to the school-to-prison pipeline; and,
- hold elected officials accountable to UN Agenda 2030, especially Target 4 ('Ensure inclusive and quality education for all and promote lifelong learning').

• International and multilateral efforts:

- reaffirm UN commitments covering the rights of children, specifically, the right to education is enshrined within the 1948 Universal Declaration of Human Rights and the 1960 UNESCO Convention against Discrimination in Education, and the rights of the child to nondiscrimination and to be protected against any form of physical or mental violence, injury or abuse is described within the 1989 Convention of the Rights of the Child;
- reaffirm the UN 2030 Agenda for Sustainable Development, especially SDG Target 4; and,
- integrate inclusive data collection into all international public health/development surveys to illustrate the impact of violence, discrimination, and exclusion on the well-being and achievement of LGBTQ+ students, as well as on the aspirations of nations for growth and economic stability.

Research and advocacy for safe and equitable access to LGBTQ+-inclusive primary and secondary schools are not only possible, but also necessary, at the local, national, and international levels. The transnational movement to counter the authoritarian backlash against education justice for LGBTQ+ youth is a necessary component of the larger struggle for education, critical thinking, and democracy for all.

Notes

[1] Meaning gender equality between women and men, and/or inclusion of transgender people in the polity.

[2] According to historian Samuel Moyn (2018), this anti-Semitic conspiracy theory, revived by the alt-right in the US and elsewhere, refers to "an unholy alliance of abortionists, feminists, globalists, homosexuals, intellectuals and socialists who have translated the far left's old campaign to take away people's privileges from 'class struggle' into 'identity politics' and multiculturalism."

[3] GLSEN previously stood for Gay, Lesbian and Straight Education Network, and the organization is now simply referred to as "GLSEN."

References

Bosia, M.J. (2013) Why states act: Homophobia and crisis. In M.L. Weiss and M.J. Bosia (eds) *Global Homophobia: States, Movements and the Politics of Oppression*. Chicago, IL: University of Illinois Press, pp 30–54.

Flores, A. (2019) Social acceptance of LGBT people in 174 countries, 1981 to 2017. The Williams Institute, Los Angeles, CA. Available at: https://williamsinstitute.law.ucla.edu/publications/global-acceptance-index-lgbt/

Hess, B. (1999) Breaking and entering the establishment: Committing social change and confronting the backlash. *Social Problems*, 46(1): 1–12.

Kosciw, J. and Pizmony-Levy, O. (2016) International perspectives on homophobic and transphobic bullying in schools. *Journal of LGBT Youth*, 13(1–2): 1–5.

Kosciw, J. and Zongrone, A. (2019) *A Global School Climate Crisis: Insights on Lesbian, Gay, Bisexual, Transgender & Queer Students in Latin America*. GLSEN: New York, NY.

Morán Faúndes, J.M. (2019) The geopolitics of noral panic: The influence of Argentinian neo-conservatism in the genesis of the discourse of 'gender ideology'. *International Sociology*, 34(4): 402–417.

Moyn, S. (2018) The alt-right's favorite meme is 100 years old. *New York Times*, November 13. Available at: www.nytimes.com/2018/11/13/opinion/cultural-marxism-anti-semitism.html

Nuñez-Mietz, F.G. (2019) Resisting human rights through securitization: Russia and Hungary against LGBT rights. *Journal of Human Rights*, 18(5): 543–563.

Payne, L. and de Souza Santos. A.A. (2020) The right-wing backlash in Brazil and beyond, *Politics & Gender* 16(1): 32–38.

Pew Research Center (2020) *The Global Divide on Homosexuality Persists*. Pew Research Center: Washington, DC.

UN (2015a) UN Agenda 2030. Resolution adopted by the General Assembly on 25 September 2015. A/RES/70/1. Available at: https://www.un.org/ga/search/view_doc.asp?symbol=A/RES/70/1&Lang=E

UN (2015b) *Ending Violence and Discrimination against Lesbian, Gay, Bisexual, Transgender and Intersex People*. New York: OHCHR.

UNESCO (2016) *Out in the Open. Education Sector Responses to Violence Based on Sexual Orientation and Gender Identity/Expression*. Paris: UNESCO. Available at: https://en.unesco.org/news/out-open-unesco-takes-school-related-homophobic-and-transphobic-violence.

UNESCO/UNGEI (2016) *Why Ending School-Related Gender-Based Violence (SRGBV) is Critical to Sustainable Development*. Available at: https://www.ungei.org/publication/why-ending-school-related-gender-based-violence-critical-sustainable-development

World Bank (2015) Sexual Orientation and Gender Identity. Washington DC: World Bank. Available at: https://www.worldbank.org/en/topic/ sexual-orientation-and-gender-identity

Further reading

Gessen, M. (2017) Why autocrats fear LGBT rights. *The New York Review of Books*, July 27. Available at: www.nybooks.com/daily/2017/07/27/ why-autocrats-fear-lgbt-rights-trump/

ILGA World (no date) State-sponsored homophobia: sexual orientation laws in the world. Available at: https://ilga.org/resources

ILGA World (no date) Trans legal mapping report: recognition before the law. Available at: https://ilga.org/resources

Kaoma, K. (2012) Exporting the anti-gay movement: how sexual minorities in Africa became collateral damage in the U.S. culture wars. *American Prospect*, April 24. Available at: https://prospect.org/world/exporting-anti-gay-movement/

Kosciw, J.G., Clark, C.M., Truong, N.L., and Zongrone, A.D. (2020) *The 2019 National School Climate Survey: The Experiences of Lesbian, Gay, Bisexual, Transgender, and Queer Youth in Our Nation's Schools*. New York, NY: GLSEN. Available at: www.glsen.org/research/2019-national-school-climate-survey

Movement Advancement Project (no date) Education. Available at: www. lgbtmap.org/education

UNESCO and UN Women (2016) Global guidance on addressing school-related gender-based violence. Available at: https://unesdoc.unesco.org/ ark:/48223/pf0000246651

From the streets to social policy: how to end gender-based violence against women

Özlem Altıok

The problem

Until the 1970s, violence against women (VAW) was framed as a private issue and remained conspicuously absent from the public sphere and policy debates. Today, owing to decades of protest by women's movements in different parts of the world, VAW—and gender-based violence (GBV) directed against lesbian, gay, bisexual, transgender, queer/questioning, intersex and other non-heteronormative (LGBTQI+) individuals—is widely recognized as a serious human rights violation and a health problem that disproportionately affects women.

Patriarchy, which subjects women and girls to violence because of their sex, is the root cause of VAW and GBV. As the 1993 UN Declaration on the Elimination of Violence Against Women (DEVAW) put it:

> [VAW] is a manifestation of historically unequal power relations between men and women, which have led to domination over and discrimination against women by men and to the prevention of the full advancement of women ... [VAW] is one of the crucial social mechanisms by which women are forced into a subordinate position compared with men.

Feminists have always challenged the private–public dichotomy, which serves to depoliticize the unequal power relations within the home, where VAW often takes place. The terms used, as discussed by Ertürk (2016), to refer to the problem are instructive of the shifts in how VAW has been framed. The First World Conference on Women in Mexico City in 1975 made reference to "unity of the family and prevention of intra-family conflicts." Five years later, at the Copenhagen Conference, a resolution on "battered women and the family" was adopted, and the concluding document made reference to "domestic violence." The first time that violence against women was framed as a global social problem was in 1985 at the civil society forum at the Nairobi Conference, whose final document, *Nairobi Forward-looking Strategies*, linked the promotion of peace with the elimination of VAW in both private and public spheres, connecting violence in the home to armed conflict situations for the first time in the international policy arena (Ertürk 2016).

Violence against women and girls (VAWG) is a violation of human rights and a form of discrimination against women: "It includes all acts of gender-based violence that result in, or are likely to result in, physical, sexual, psychological or economic harm or suffering to women, including threats of such acts, coercion or arbitrary deprivation of liberty, whether occurring in public or in private life" (UN, 1993). The Istanbul Convention, the most comprehensive treaty specifically about VAW, defines "gender-based violence against women" as "violence that is directed against a woman because she is a woman or that affects women disproportionately" (Council of Europe, 2011).

The most extreme case of violence against women is *femicide or feminicide*, defined as the killing of women and girls because of their gender. Latin American feminists coined *"femicidio"* in response to an alarming escalation of very violent murders of women and girls. In parallel, the term *"feminicidio"* was introduced to capture the element of impunity and institutional violence owing to a lack of accountability and adequate response on the part of the state.

Despite the achievements and diversity of the women's and, more recently, LGBTQI+ movements, patriarchal power relations—even when destabilized or relatively tamed—continue to reproduce gendered discrimination and provoke violence. Furthermore, VAW is aggravated in times of economic, environmental, health, and other crises. Race, ethnicity, class, and immigration status shape women's vulnerability to, and experiences of, violence. In addition to the political-economic factors that lead to VAW, recent research suggests that increases in VAW signal impending social and economic crises.

Research evidence

VAW is a universally prevalent problem, even in countries where women's legal rights are safeguarded. Globally, one in three women of reproductive age have experienced physical and/or sexual interpersonal violence (IPV) in their lifetime.

Only a few comprehensive cross-country surveys on VAW exist. Of these, the European Union (EU) Agency for Fundamental Rights' (FRA, 2014) "Violence against women survey" (conducted in 2014 in 28 member states) and the Organization for Security and Cooperation's (OSCE's) survey (conducted in 2018 in seven member countries) both find the prevalence of violence by an intimate partner to be around 22 per cent. They also find low (~15 per cent) reporting rates, particularly when perpetrators are current partners. The OSCE survey reports the prevalence of violence at around 20 per cent for the general population and higher among women who: have disabilities (22 per cent); work without pay in family businesses (27 per cent); and are in poverty, who typically have less control over household decision-making (32 per cent).

Forms of VAW

VAW can take four main forms: physical, sexual, economic, and psychological/emotional (see Figure 3.1). These can take place in the family and within communities, and can be perpetrated directly or condoned by the state.

Prevalence of VAW and data sources

The World Health Organization's (WHO's) *Multi-country Study on Women's Health and Domestic Violence against Women* (Garcia Moreno et al, 2005) shows that the proportion of the female population subjected to IPV ranges from 15 to 71 per cent (see Figure 3.2). Only a minority (5 to 45 per cent) of survivors report victimization. According to a nationally representative survey conducted in Turkey in 2015, for example, about 40 per cent of women suffer from physical and/or sexual violence in that country but only 11 per cent of them report it to the police or other authorities (Yüksel Kaptanoğlu et al, 2015).

Besides surveys, VAW data also come from crime statistics collected by the police and courts. These show that, globally, 38.6 per cent of female homicides are committed by an intimate partner (versus only 6.3 per cent of male homicides). Separation and estrangements are the primary motives. Perpetrators of femicides usually use weapons (72.6 per cent of femicide cases in Portugal; 79.4 per cent in Italy; 83.4 per cent in Turkey). The risk of femicide is independent of the race/ethnicity of either abuser or victim but increases by 500 per cent when the abuser has access to firearms.

Risk factors associated with IPV

Not all men are perpetrators of VAW. Individuals' past histories, current family relations, and community-level influences, as well as social-structural context, matter. Heise's ecological framework (Heise 1998 cited in Moreno et al. 2005) explains VAW by reference to societal, community, family, and individual contexts, highlighting some common risk factors, including: norms and laws granting men control over women's behavior and the acceptability of violence for resolving conflict; the existence of armed conflict

Figure 3.1: VAW forms, examples, and life cycle

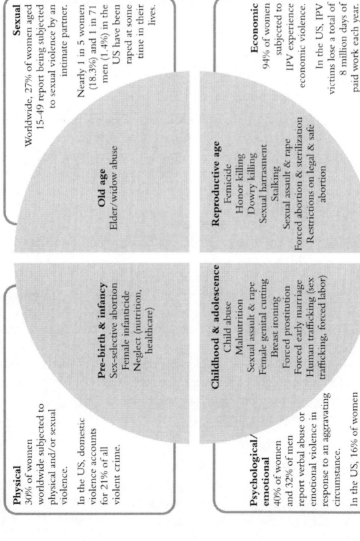

Physical
30% of women worldwide subjected to physical and/or sexual violence.

In the US, domestic violence accounts for 21% of all violent crime.

Sexual
Worldwide, 27% of women aged 15–49 report being subjected to sexual violence by an intimate partner.

Nearly 1 in 5 women (18.3%) and 1 in 71 men (1.4%) in the US have been raped at some time in their lives.

Economic
94% of women subjected to IPV experience economic violence.

In the US, IPV victims lose a total of 8 million days of paid work each year.

Old age
Elder/widow abuse

Reproductive age
Femicide
Honor killing
Dowry killing
Sexual harassment
Stalking
Sexual assault & rape
Forced abortion & sterilization
Restrictions on legal & safe abortion

Pre-birth & infancy
Sex-selective abortion
Female infanticide
Neglect (nutrition, healthcare)

Childhood & adolescence
Child abuse
Malnutrition
Sexual assault & rape
Female genital cutting
Breast ironing
Forced prostitution
Forced early marriage
Human trafficking (sex trafficking, forced labor)

Psychological/ emotional
40% of women and 32% of men report verbal abuse or emotional violence in response to an aggravating circumstance.

In the US, 16% of women and 5% of men report being victimized by stalking.

Sources: Garcia Moreno et al (2005), Ellsberg and Heise (2005), CDC (2010)

Figure 3.2: VAW prevalence in selected countries

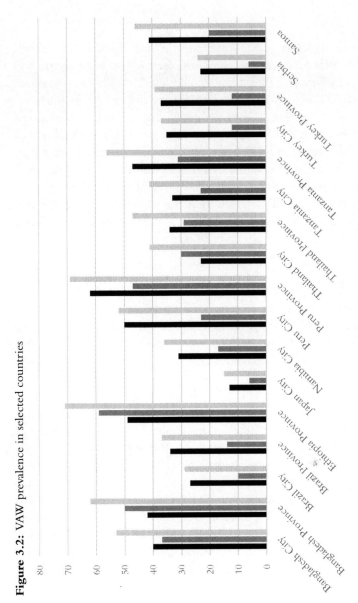

■ % women who have ever experienced physical violence by a partner

▨ % women who have ever experienced sexual violence by a partner

▨ % women who have ever experienced physical and/or sexual violence by a partner

Sources: Ellsberg and Heise (2005) and Yüksel Kaptanoglu et al (2015)

and generalized violence; women's and familial isolation, delinquent peer groups, and low socio-economic status; marital conflict, male control of wealth and decision-making, poverty, and unemployment; and being male, witnessing marital conflict as a child, and being abused as a child.

Health consequences

VAW causes serious short- and long-term physical, mental, sexual, and reproductive health problems for women, leading to high social and economic costs for women, their families, and societies. These can include fatal outcomes (like homicide or suicide) or injuries, unintended pregnancies, induced abortions, gynecological problems, and sexually transmitted infections, including HIV. IPV during pregnancy increases the likelihood of miscarriage, stillbirth, pre-term delivery, and low birthweight. It can lead to depression, post-traumatic stress and other anxiety disorders, sleep difficulties, eating disorders, suicide attempts, and poor overall health. Sexual violence, particularly during childhood, can lead to increased smoking, substance use, and risky sexual behaviors. It is also associated with perpetration of violence (for males) and being a victim of violence (for females).

Impact on children

Growing up amid familial violence may lead to behavioral and emotional disturbances for children, and these are associated with perpetrating or experiencing violence later in life. IPV is also associated with higher rates of infant and child mortality and morbidity.

VAW during the COVID-19 pandemic

VAW has been described as the "shadow pandemic." Early in the COVID-19 pandemic, UN Women (2020) estimated that the number of women and girls aged 15–49 who were subjected to physical and/or sexual violence in the previous 12 months (243 million) would likely increase. Evidence from numerous countries indicates that under "stay at home" orders and "lockdown" measures, VAW has increased and/or intensified. Policies that specifically and further limited access to abortion services during the pandemic added to women's burden. LGBTQI+ organizations have also reported increased demand for their services.

Recommendations and solutions

The solutions to the problem of VAW lie in adopting and implementing social policies designed to transform historically unequal power relations that force women into a subordinate position relative to men. There are three structural elements within which VAW should be seen and addressed.

First, the gendered division of labor in the home and women's unpaid care work restricts women's education, employment, and retirement opportunities, as well as limiting their participation in politics. Social policies that remove barriers to women's access to education, paid work, and political participation should be adopted so that problems that affect women disproportionately can be taken seriously and addressed effectively. These policies include publicly provided childcare, paid parental leave, and electoral gender quotas.

Second, neoliberal globalization has increased employment opportunities for women, but women are overrepresented in low-wage jobs that do not offer decent work conditions and suffer from a gender pay gap. Without a reduction in the unpaid care work women tend to do in their home— their "second shift"—women's increased participation in the labor force has resulted in an intensification of work and exploitation. Furthermore, reductions in public services, such as education and healthcare, have disproportionate impacts on women, who bear much of the burden of privatization and rollbacks in publicly provided services (for example, caring for students with special needs and providing in-home care for patients and those who cannot take care of themselves). Such policies as a universal basic income and universal healthcare would reduce the care burden that disproportionately falls on women and empower them economically and socially.

Third, armed conflict and war, often related to power and productive resources, normalize violence and spread it throughout society. Research shows that state- and group-sanctioned violence often celebrates masculine aggression and perpetuates impunity with regard to men's violence against women. Conflict, war, and the security agenda impoverish societies, as they make trade-offs between military spending and spending for development and human rights protection, particularly that of women. A feminist foreign policy, entailing a universal reduction in states' military spending and a concomitant increase in gender-sensitive budgets that aim for just and egalitarian societies, should be adopted. Women's and other marginalized groups' experiences and knowledge should be reflected in public spending priorities and represented in the conceptualization and realization of sustainable and inclusive peace.

The policy framework just outlined would foster a politics of equal participation in the home, in workplaces, and in political life, and would empower women in ways that radically reorder patriarchal capitalism. In addition, there are three specific solutions to ending VAW:

- upholding and adopting universal legal standards to ensure gender equality and prevent VAW;
- strengthening the effective implementation of commitments at the national level; and
- collecting sex-segregated data on VAW, LGBTQI+ individuals, and children.

International and regional treaties to end VAW

In the absence of a comprehensive and binding global treaty specifically on VAW, one solution to ending VAW lies in the effective implementation of the 1979 United Nations (UN) Convention on the Elimination of all Forms of Discrimination Against Women (CEDAW). CEDAW establishes the main international framework to end discrimination against women, including, by implication, VAW. Ratified by 189 countries, CEDAW has since adopted Recommendations No. 12 (in 1989), No. 19 (in 1992), and No. 35 (in 2017), which urge states to specifically address the structural causes of GBV against women and adopt concrete measures to end it.

States can also adopt one of three notable regional treaties aiming specifically to end VAW: the Inter-American Convention on the Prevention, Punishment, and Eradication of Violence against Women (Belém do Pará Convention, effective 1995); the Protocol to the African Charter on Human and Peoples' Rights on the Rights of Women in Africa (Moputo Protocol, effective 2005); and the Council of Europe Convention on Preventing and Combating Violence Against Women and Domestic Violence (Istanbul Convention, effective 2014). The Istanbul Convention and the Belém do Pará Convention, in particular, explicitly address the relationship between gender inequality and violence, and obligate states to establish comprehensive national legal and educational systems to prevent VAW. These treaties are important for the conceptualization of VAW, which should guide data-collection processes at the national level. They also have specific stipulations for the establishment of rape crisis centers and shelters, as well as other support services needed by survivors of violence. Both conventions have been ratified by a majority of the states in their respective regions and have helped create or strengthen national mechanisms to prevent VAW. In addition, feminist organizations are currently advocating for the EU to adopt the Istanbul Convention. Even where a comprehensive regional treaty applies, however, there are problems in implementation, even in those states where laws have been passed and institutions established to address VAW.

National legislation to end VAW and its effective implementation

National laws should be put in place to eliminate legal and cultural practices that condone VAW, and such laws should be effectively implemented in line with the universal principles of equality and nondiscrimination. For example, the definition and prosecution of rape should be clear and should not exclude marital rape. Reductions in sentences for rapists who marry their victims should be eliminated. Similarly, there should be no reduced sentences in criminal codes for perpetrators of femicide who claim to have killed women in the name of "honor." In cases where VAW is of a systematic nature, it should be regarded and prosecuted as torture and cruel, inhuman, and degrading treatment or punishment. To complement prevention and protection efforts, punishment that deters potential perpetrators of VAW is needed.

The proverbial wheel need not be reinvented when it comes to what kinds of policies should guide national legislation. The Istanbul Convention is seen as the gold standard in setting out specific measures and placing concrete obligations on states to prevent VAW. International efforts to end VAW will need to draw on the convention's strengths, including the concrete measures for prevention, protection, prosecution, and integrated policies that the convention lays out (for a summary, see Figure 3.3).

A vital issue that needs to be addressed, and that disproportionately affects women, is the widespread tendency of police and other public officials to consider VAW cases as "family matters." This can be ameliorated by training law enforcement, prosecutors, and judges so that they apply and implement the principles of due diligence and nondiscrimination in cases of VAW, and so that they also know about and can direct survivors to specialized medical, psychological, social, and legal support services for women in situations of violence. Other initiatives that some countries have taken include the establishment of specialized police services and courts to deal with VAW and domestic violence.

Many women's rights organizations around the world engage in public campaigns to raise awareness to end VAW. Their efforts should be supported by public and private institutions. In addition, it is vital to train journalists, reporters, and other media professionals to ensure that the language and visuals they use in reporting VAW do not blame victims/survivors, justify VAW, or reproduce common misconceptions about the nature of the problem.

National and global data collection

International surveys, such as the WHO's Multi-country Study on Women's Health and Domestic Violence against Women, the International VAW

Figure 3.3: The 4 Ps of the 2011 Istanbul Convention

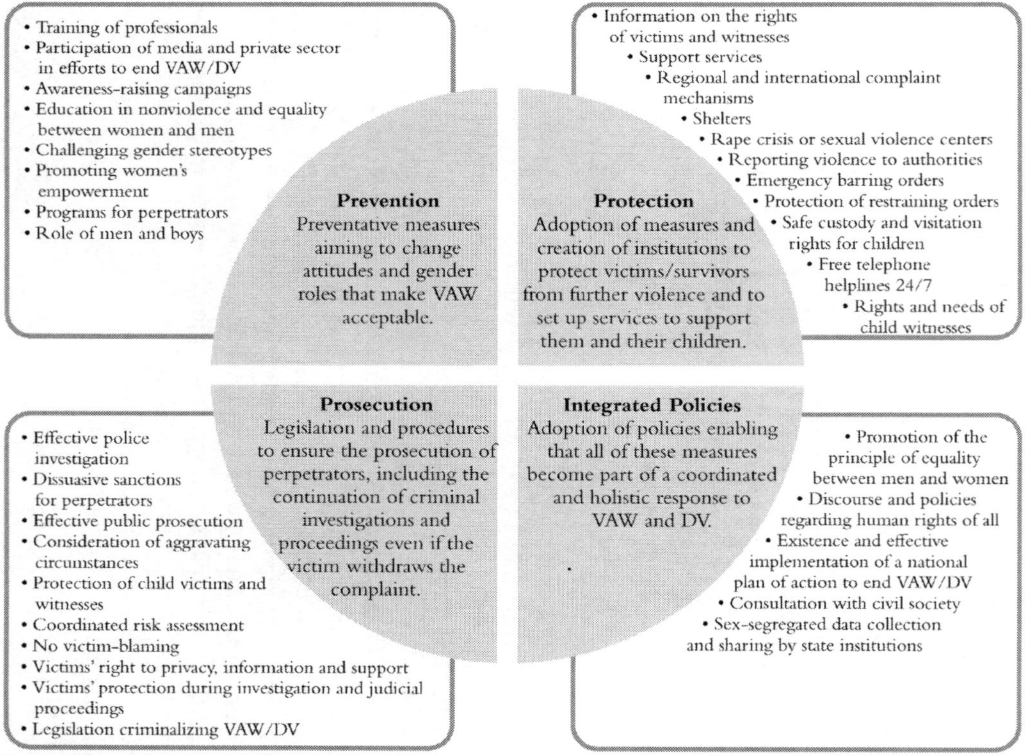

Prevention
Preventative measures aiming to change attitudes and gender roles that make VAW acceptable.

- Training of professionals
- Participation of media and private sector in efforts to end VAW/DV
- Awareness-raising campaigns
- Education in nonviolence and equality between women and men
- Challenging gender stereotypes
- Promoting women's empowerment
- Programs for perpetrators
- Role of men and boys

Protection
Adoption of measures and creation of institutions to protect victims/survivors from further violence and to set up services to support them and their children.

- Information on the rights of victims and witnesses
- Support services
  - Regional and international complaint mechanisms
  - Shelters
  - Rape crisis or sexual violence centers
  - Reporting violence to authorities
  - Emergency barring orders
  - Protection of restraining orders
  - Safe custody and visitation rights for children
  - Free telephone helplines 24/7
  - Rights and needs of child witnesses

Prosecution
Legislation and procedures to ensure the prosecution of perpetrators, including the continuation of criminal investigations and proceeding even if the victim withdraws the complaint.

- Effective police investigation
- Dissuasive sanctions for perpetrators
- Effective public prosecution
- Consideration of aggravating circumstances
- Protection of child victims and witnesses
- Coordinated risk assessment
- No victim-blaming
- Victims' right to privacy, information and support
- Victims' protection during investigation and judicial proceedings
- Legislation criminalizing VAW/DV

Integrated Policies
Adoption of policies enabling that all of these measures become part of a coordinated and holistic response to VAW and DV.

- Promotion of the principle of equality between men and women
- Discourse and policies regarding human rights of all
- Existence and effective implementation of a national plan of action to end VAW/DV
- Consultation with civil society
- Sex-segregated data collection and sharing by state institutions

Note: DV = domestic violence.

Source: Istanbul Convention Infographics, available at: https://rm.coe.int/coe-istanbulconvention-infografic-en-r04-v01/1680a06d0d

Survey (IVAWS), and the USA's demographic and health surveys (DHS) and multi-indicator cluster surveys (MICS), provide some comparative data. However, the extent of VAW is currently hidden.

Accurate and representative data are needed to measure VAW over time. With the possible exception of homicide rates, administrative data underrepresent the real occurrence of VAW. Statistical authorities need to revise their categories for data and indicators in order to align with recent developments in international law, public policy, and scholarly research. Such data should be using the same categories to measure the extent and severity of violence in both surveys and the various administrative sources. This is important to ensure that data are comparable across different agencies within a given country and, ideally, to facilitate comparisons across countries. Attention needs to be paid to the statistical categories used nationally as well as internationally by the UN (Sustainable Development Goals [SDGs], UN Office of Drug and Crime, UN Women, the WHO, and UN Statistical Commission) and in Europe (Eurostat, European Sourcebook, and European Institute for Gender Equality).

Existing statistics that can be used as indicators of the real rate of VAW and its change over time are femicide (gender-disaggregated homicide), domestic violent crime, and conviction rates for homicide and rape. Generally, the framework to measure VAW requires attention to violence, gender, and measurement and counting rules. As Walby et al (2017) explain, both *actions (and intentions)* and *harm/injury (and lack of consent)* should be included, and *different types of violence* should be specified. On gender, the sex of the victim and the perpetrator, the relationship of victim to perpetrator, whether there was a sexual dimension to the violence, and whether there was a gender motivation should be part of measurement. Three units of measurement should be used at the same time: the event, victim, and perpetrator (along with data on age, the temporality of violence, and what the counting/reporting rules are when multiple crimes and/or victims and perpetrators exist).

Given that different administrative agencies collect data for their different purposes, there are some challenges to coordination at the national level. Nevertheless, research on VAW demonstrates that it is necessary to incorporate and make visible the gendered nature of violence in crime statistics, as well as to ensure that the crime statistics can in some way be made compatible with health statistics.

On femicides in particular, there should be data collection both at national levels and in the form of a global observatory. One of the main priorities is to collect sex-segregated data in all countries. Globally, 13.5 per cent of homicides are committed by an intimate partner, and this figure is higher for intentional homicides. The significance of sex-segregated data—which are collected in some national crime statistics, but not all—is evident when we consider that globally, 38.6 per cent of female homicides are committed by an intimate partner (compared to only 6.3 per cent of male homicides being committed by intimate partners). Similarly, sex-segregated data on motives might differ by sex/gender.

Contemporary challenges and ongoing struggles

A notable challenge standing in the way of ending VAW is right-wing populism and the rise of authoritarian governments in Europe and elsewhere. These are now contesting multilateralism, international commitments on ending VAW, and the very principle of gender equality. The most striking example of this came in 2021, when Turkey, the first country to have signed the Istanbul Convention in 2011, announced its withdrawal from it by a presidential decision. This unprecedented (and unconstitutional) move has been resisted by the women's movement in Turkey, which continues to challenge the president's decision in court, demonstrating the dynamic relationship between feminist struggles and social policy.

Nevertheless, Turkey's withdrawal is likely to embolden other right-wing authoritarian governments and movements in Europe (for example, in Poland and Hungary) that have been attacking the convention on the grounds that it imposes a "gender ideology," undermines "traditional values," and promotes homosexuality. These movements and governments also use religious and cultural arguments to contest the consensus reached on women's human rights, the rule of law, and democracy.

While most of the current focus in dealing with the problem of VAW is on the effective implementation of existing legal instruments, a feminist education in unlearning and disrupting oppressive and exploitative gender relations is crucial for transforming patriarchal cultures. Feminist concepts, discourse, practice, and social policy are vital for a radical reordering of patriarchal capitalism, which breeds violence in interpersonal relationships, in communities, and between polities.

References

Black, M.C., Basile, K.C., Breiding, M.J., Smith, S.G., Walters, M.L., Merrick, M.T., Chen, J., and Stevens, M.R. (2011) The National Intimate Partner and Sexual Violence Survey (NISVS): 2010 Summary Report. Atlanta, GA: National Center for Injury Prevention and Control, Centers for Disease Control and Prevention.

Council of Europe (2011) *The Council of Europe Convention on Preventing and Combating Violence against Women and Domestic Violence.* Available at https://rm.coe.int/168008482e

Ellsberg, M. and Heise, L. (2005) *Researching Violence against Women: A Practical Guide for Researchers and Activists*. Washington, DC: World Health Organization and PATH.

Ertürk, Y. (2016) *Violence without Borders: Paradigm, Policy and Praxis Concerning Violence against Women*. Washington, DC: Women's Learning Partnership.

FRA (European Union Agency for Fundamental Rights) (2014) Violence against women: an EU-wide survey. Available at: https://fra.europa.eu/sites/default/files/fra_uploads/fra-2014-vaw-survey-main-results-apr14_en.pdf

Garcia-Moreno, C., Jansen, H., Ellsberg, M., Heise, L., and Watts, C. (2005) *WHO Multi-country Study on Women's Health and Domestic Violence against Women*, Geneva: World Health Organization.

United Nations Declaration on the Elimination of Violence against Women (1993). Available at https://www.un.org/en/genocideprevention/documents/atrocity-crimes/Doc.21_declaration%20elimination%20vaw.pdf

UN Women (2020) Violence against women and girls: the shadow pandemic. Available at: https://www.unwomen.org/en/news/stories/2020/4/statement-ed-phumzile-violence-against-women-during-pandemic

Walby, S., Towers, J., Balderston, S., Corradi, C., Francis, B. Heiskanen, M., Helweg-Larsen, K., Mergaert, L., Olive, P., Kelly, E., Stöckl, H. and Strid, S. (2017) *The Concept and Measurement of Violence against Women and Men*. Bristol: Policy Press.

Yüksel Kaptanoğlu, I., Çavlin, A. and Akadlı Ergöçmen, B. (2015) Research on domestic violence against women in Turkey. Hacettepe University Institute of Population Studies. Available at: www.openaccess.hacettepe.edu.tr:8080/xmlui/handle/11655/23338

Further reading

Altıok, Ö. (2021) Turkey's withdrawal from the Istanbul Convention: a threshold we better not cross. Forum EU. Available at: https://esikplatform.net/kategori/haberler/72169/turkey-s-withdrawal-from-the-istanbul-convention-a-threshold-we-better-not-cross

Devries, K.M., Mak, J.Y.T., García-Moreno, C., Petzold, M., Child, J.C., Falder, G., Lim, S., Bacchus, L.J., Engell, R.E., Rosenfeld, L., Pallitto, C., Vos, T., Abrahams, N. and Watts, C. H. (2013) The global prevalence of intimate partner violence against women. *Science*, 340(6140): 1527–8.

Krantz, G. and Garcia-Moreno, C. (2005) Violence against women. *Journal of Epidemiology & Community Health* 59: 818–21. Available at: https://jech.bmj.com/content/jech/59/10/818.full.pdf

Menjivar, C. and Salcido, O. (2002) Immigrant women and domestic violence: common experiences in different countries. *Gender & Society*, 16(6): 898–920.

Peterman, A. and O'Donnell, M. (2021) COVID-19 and violence against women and children: a second research round up. Center for Global Development, September 23. Available at: www.cgdev.org/publication/covid-19-and-violence-against-women-and-children-second-research-round

Reid, G. (2021) Global trends in LGBT rights during the Covid-19 pandemic. Human Rights Watch. Available at: www.hrw.org/news/2021/02/24/global-trends-lgbt-rights-during-covid-19-pandemic

Šimonović, D. (2021) Rape as a grave, systematic and widespread human rights violation, a crime and manifestation of gender-based violence against women and girls, and its prevention. United Nations. Available at: https://undocs.org/A/HRC/47/26

True, J. (2012) The Political Economy of Violence against Women. Oxford University Press.

Women's Platform for Equality, Turkey (EŞİK) Available at https://esikplatform.net/

World Health Organization (2018) Violence against women prevalence estimates, 2018. Available at: www.who.int/publications/i/item/9789240022256

FOUR

Fatphobia

Laurie Cooper Stoll, Angela Meadows, Stephanie von Liebenstein, and Carina Elisabeth Carlsen

The problem

Fatphobia—that is, the fear, hatred, and loathing of fat bodies—is pervasive worldwide. Studies show that fat people experience discrimination in employment, education, media, interpersonal relationships, politics, and especially healthcare. Fatphobia starts young and runs deep; fatphobic attitudes have been recorded in children as young as three and become more pronounced with age. Cross-cultural studies confirm that socialization to fatphobia is not limited to North American populations. Data from the Project Implicit study, including over 300,000 respondents from 71 nations, demonstrate consistent pro-thin, anti-fat biases. A recent examination of longitudinal trends in prejudicial attitudes toward a range of stigmatized groups found that between 2007 and 2016, both explicit fatphobic attitudes (for example, acknowledging a preference for thin people over fat people) and implicit fatphobic attitudes (for example, associating negative words and phrases with images of fat people) either remained stable or increased, while stigma toward many other oppressed groups showed a downward trajectory.

Despite these findings, fatphobia is rarely seen as an important social justice issue and global social problem. This is because, unlike other marginalized identities, we are taught to see being fat as a "choice," specifically, a *bad* choice. In many countries, fat bodies are viewed exclusively through medical and public health discourses that label fat bodies as diseased and therefore in need of prevention, intervention, and cure, regardless of the risks involved. This creates an environment in which fat people are blamed for their own oppression and makes it socially acceptable to censure, intimidate, harass, and discriminate against fat people because of their weight. It also frames fat exclusively as an individual-level problem, as opposed to a structural or social problem: fat people are seen as "the problem," while fatphobic policies, practices, and institutions that regularly harm fat people are seen as acceptable or even justified.

The evidence

Due to fatphobia, fat people experience stigma and discrimination across multiple domains of daily life, including education, paid work, and healthcare. When it comes to education, weight-related bullying in schools is widespread and exceeds rates of bullying for race, sexuality, academic performance, and physical disability. The international Health Behavior in School-aged Children study, comprising nationally representative samples of over 200,000 adolescents from 39 North American and European countries and regions, found that fat children were up to twice as likely as thin children to be the targets of chronic bullying. These negative experiences have been linked to lower engagement in school activities and increased truancy, and are associated with increased risk of depression, substance use, eating disorders, and suicidality.

Fat children also shoulder a penalty in academic achievement at every level of education, receiving lower grades than their non-fat peers, despite no difference in scores on tests of academic or intellectual ability. Furthermore, fat students show lower rates of enrollment in postsecondary education, perform less well, and are less likely to graduate than their thinner peers. For many of these outcomes, the weight penalty is more severe for female children. In sum, by the end of their formal education, some fat students may already be faced with fewer opportunities for success in life simply because they matriculated through the educational system at a higher weight.

These disadvantages and disparities in opportunity continue to widen after fat people leave school. When it comes to employment, fat people experience discrimination at every point in their life trajectories. Fat people are less likely to be hired, less likely to receive positive evaluations or be promoted, and more likely to be disciplined or wrongfully terminated at paid work. A Body Mass Index (BMI) wage penalty has been consistently demonstrated in research studies worldwide and appears to be worsening over time. Data from a nationally representative sample of nearly 3,000 US citizens highlight that discrimination increased exponentially with each higher BMI category, and data from a French national sample indicate that "obese" individuals spend more years unemployed than "non-obese" individuals and are less likely to find work after a period of unemployment. In almost all cases, the weight penalty is more severe for women than men, and women begin to experience discrimination at a much lower BMI threshold than men. Thus, while men experience fatphobia, fat women—and even more so, fat women who are also members of other historically marginalized groups—experience greater discrimination resulting from overlapping domains of oppression.

Fatphobia has also been documented across numerous specialties in healthcare, including, for example, in the attitudes of primary care physicians, gynecologists and obstetricians, pediatricians, nurses, pharmacists, nutritionists and dietitians, psychotherapists, and physiotherapists. This includes providers specializing in the care of higher-weight patients. Anti-fat bias on the part of healthcare workers leads to differential treatment of fat patients in healthcare settings, which explains why fat patients consistently report dissatisfaction with healthcare interactions. Some even report blatantly hostile or offensive treatment. In addition, fear of experiencing fatphobia in healthcare means that fat patients are more likely to avoid healthcare settings altogether, especially when their situation is nonurgent. As a case in point, fat women tend to have higher rates of certain types of gynecological cancers. While this is often attributed to their body weight, data show that fat women are less likely to get preventive screenings for these cancers, even when they have insurance, due to the harassment they experience about their weight when they go to the doctor. Even when care is accessed, inappropriate or even negligent care is common, sometimes with fatal results. Indeed, there are many documented cases of fat people dying from serious diseases because their healthcare providers did not take their concerns seriously.

The solution

Before considering how we can address the pervasiveness of fatphobia around the globe, we first need to acknowledge that the rejection of fatness is something that is deeply anchored in our cultures, not only in the Global North (for example, the US, the UK, Canada, and Western European nations), but also increasingly in countries and cultures where fat bodies have previously been valued, like the Pacific Islands, sub-Saharan Africa, and the West Indies. Eliminating fatphobia will not be easy and will require a multilevel approach. We focus on three broad areas that are strong targets for initial interventions: (1) education; (2) public health; and (3) policies and laws.

Education

With children as young as three demonstrating anti-fat attitudes, and with children as young as five being hospitalized for eating disorders, efforts to reduce fatphobia must start early. One place children learn fatphobic attitudes is schools. To combat fatphobia, school districts should eliminate any policies, practices, and/or curricula that equate weight with health and frame weight control as a health behavior. However well intentioned, such programs reinforce fatphobic attitudes and can promote disordered eating, even giving rise to clinical eating disorders. When required by law, school wellness programs should be based on weight-neutral approaches, such as the principles of Health at Every Size®. As outlined by the Association for Size Diversity and Health (ASDAH), Health at Every Size® principles include: (1) accepting and respecting the inherent diversity of body shapes and sizes; (2) supporting health policies that improve and equalize access to information and services, as well as personal practices that improve human well-being; (3) promoting flexible, individualized eating based on hunger, satiety, nutritional needs, and pleasure, rather than any externally regulated eating plan focused on weight control; (4) supporting physical activities that allow people of all sizes, abilities, and interests to engage in enjoyable movement to the degree that they choose; and (5) acknowledging our biases, understanding the overlap with other forms of stigma (for example, racism and classism), and working to end weight discrimination and the broader societal inequalities that feed into it.

Where school wellness programs are mandated, they should also include media literacy training that promotes an inclusive view of all body types. Teaching children and adolescents how to think critically about what they see in the media and the messages that accompany those images is imperative given that exposure to media, particularly social media, is consistently linked with negative body image. Studies show that media literacy can be effective at reducing body dissatisfaction and disordered eating in younger adolescents. Children should also be encouraged to appreciate body size diversity. Fortunately, there are several weight-inclusive, body-positive books for children of all ages that are now available, as well as weight-neutral curricula for high schools and universities focused on reducing body dissatisfaction. For example, the Be Body Positive Model in the US focuses on five core competencies: (1) reclaiming health; (2) practicing intuitive self-care; (3) cultivating self-love; (4) declaring your own authentic beauty; and (5) building community.

We must also support legislation that prevents fatphobia in schools. In the US, the Eating Disorder Prevention in Schools Bill was introduced in the House of Representatives in 2020. This bill requires school districts that participate in school lunch or breakfast programs to: (1) include goals for reducing disordered eating in children of all sizes in their local school wellness policies; and (2) include registered dietitians and licensed mental health professionals in the development, implementation, and review of such policies. It also requires the US Department of Agriculture to assist school districts in establishing healthy school environments that promote eating disorder prevention and encourage screening for such disorders. No action has been taken on this bill to date, which points to the need to elect people to public office, including to school boards, who understand that fat is a social justice and a human rights issue, and will work to eliminate fatphobia in schools and throughout society.

Finally, a critical weight studies curriculum should be a part of any college or university degree that already considers other forms of prejudice and oppression. Yet, few universities in the world offer fat studies coursework at the undergraduate or graduate level, despite the fact that most academic experts who have helped create "critical weight studies" teach and research in these environments. Those faculty who do offer such coursework risk pushback from students, other faculty, and external sources, with potential implications for their professional advancement. Public outrage by conservative media outlets toward faculty who teach such courses and the universities that offer them has been well documented. These responses are rooted in the very fatphobia such courses are designed to challenge. Offering fat studies and body politics coursework, and creating a system of support for those who teach them, is a necessity if we wish to raise awareness about the pervasiveness of fatphobia and work to develop collective solutions to address it.

Public health

When it comes to addressing fatphobia in public health, we need to shift the focus away from problematizing fat bodies to problematizing fatphobia. Ceasing to run blatantly fatphobic public health campaigns is an important first step. Indeed, public health campaigns do not need to mention weight at all. An excellent example of this strategy is provided by Sport England's "This Girl Can" campaign, which sought to increase participation in physically active pursuits and formalized sports for women and girls of all ages, ethnicities, ability statuses, and sizes. Financed by National Lottery funds in the UK, Sport England invested in a massive, nationwide, multimedia approach and engaged with numerous corporate, media, community, and other partners to deliver their body-inclusive message. Additionally, instructions for local authorities, fitness clubs, and others who want to use the brand specifically state that weight should not be included as an influencing factor or outcome, reinforcing the message that health and well-being are not about weight. Appreciation of body functionality (versus appearance) has been shown to reduce fatphobia, and by normalizing physical activity for all bodies, this campaign attempts to negate anti-fat stereotypes and further the message that all bodies are good bodies.

Coursework in critical weight studies is also imperative for any program that trains healthcare professionals. Several studies have demonstrated that even brief exposure to materials challenging the dominant public health messaging around weight can be effective in reducing anti-fat attitudes, as well as increasing awareness of weight stigma as a social justice issue and the desire to engage in advocacy efforts more broadly. Professional organizations in health-related fields can play a role in addressing fatphobia and other forms of widespread bias and discrimination by requiring ongoing training as part of their members' licensing requirements.

While a few organizations now provide anti-weight bias resources for healthcare professionals, the most well-known perhaps being the Rudd

Center at the University of Connecticut, most trainings tend to focus on recognizing individual-level fatphobia in clinical encounters, rather than acknowledging fatphobia as a social justice issue. In contrast, such programs as Be Nourished in the US and Well Now in the UK go beyond remedying anti-fat attitudes among individual healthcare providers and toward recognizing the embeddedness of fatphobia in society and focusing on change at both the individual and structural level. These organizations offer training for providers (and certification in the case of Be Nourished) that is embedded in weight-inclusive, trauma-informed, and social justice-oriented care. Furthermore, truly impactful solutions are more likely to emerge when curriculum development involves people who are conducting research, teaching classes, and/or engaged in activism that is focused on ending fatphobia from a global perspective.

One final recommendation relates to research funding. Hundreds of millions of dollars continue to be spent on the "war on obesity," with little evidence of improvements in population health. Furthermore, the evidence supporting a shift away from a weight-centric public health paradigm is mounting. While a growing body of scholarship has pointed to the potential benefits of weight-neutral approaches to health, this avenue of research does not yet have access to the seemingly unlimited funding available for research related to obesity prevention and treatment. Funding bodies should consider allocating additional money for rigorous exploration of weight-neutral approaches. Such funding would enable larger trials, longer follow-up periods, and the development and evaluation of scalable intervention programs. These research endeavors are needed if the weight-neutral perspective is to grow beyond a niche practice into feasible and sustainable public health policies that eliminate fatphobia and promote health equity for all.

Policies and laws

In addition to addressing fatphobia in education and public health, we also need to enact policies and laws that protect fat people from discrimination. Currently, there are only two states in the US (Michigan and Washington) and a few US cities, such as San Francisco, Santa Cruz, Binghamton, and Washington DC, that have antidiscrimination laws based on weight. In the Australian state of Victoria, physical appearance is legally protected from discrimination. However, there is no country in the world with a national law that reliably protects fat people from discrimination. In the absence of these laws, some have tried to file claims of weight discrimination based on disability discrimination law, but this has rarely been successful because fatness is not typically defined as a disability.

A suitable law to prevent anti-fat discrimination would need to prohibit discrimination on the grounds of "weight" or "fatness." Given the irrefutable evidence that fatphobia causes significant harm and drives inequality, a good case could be made for adding "weight" as a distinct status within antidiscrimination law, not unlike race or gender, for example. However, given the pervasiveness of fatphobia, it may be more politically expedient, as well as more inclusive, to ban discrimination on the grounds of "height, weight, or appearance."

German activists have tirelessly pushed politicians to include an extra discrimination ground called "weight" in federal and state antidiscrimination laws. Before the federal election in 2017, the German Association Against Weight Discrimination campaigned for an inclusion of weight in the General Equal Treatment Act. Their efforts included creating an election touchstone campaign with discrimination-related questions across all discrimination categories. Activists exerted pressure on every major political party to publicly acknowledge their position on these issues. These questions and answers were made public, and the election touchstone campaign is now an ongoing project during state elections.

A suitable antidiscrimination law that protects fat people should also include a right to positive action. This would guarantee that fat people have a right not only to equal treatment (for example, in the workplace), but also to suitable accommodations (for example, an accessible office chair). Furthermore, a collective right of action and a right of representation should be instituted in countries where these do not currently exist. These legal tools ensure that fat people can collectively sue a corporation for discrimination and that an individual fat person who experiences discrimination can transfer their claim to an antidiscrimination organization or nongovernmental organization (NGO) that pursues the claim on behalf of the victim. We also need to address everyday legal practices that present fatness as a sign of human failure, situating fat people as uneducated, lazy, and/or morally deficient. Addressing fatphobia in legal practice is imperative if we want discrimination victims to feel safe to bring their claims before the court.

Finally, legislation change at the national level is often slow, but gains can be made in the meantime at state and local levels. For example, the city of Reykjavik in Iceland includes body size in the list of protected characteristics in its human rights policy. The policy not only bans overt discrimination, but also acknowledges the risks of unintentional discrimination and identifies strategies that should be implemented to reduce such risk. Understanding the city's role as a public authority, employer, and provider of services to its population, Reykjavik officials require that weight diversity be considered when making policy decisions and in service provisions, and that NGOs concerned with body respect must be consulted when their input may be relevant.

Conclusion

Eliminating fatphobia must begin with an understanding that fat is not a medical or public health crisis; rather, fat is a social justice issue. We have identified several potential avenues where progress could be made in this quest. We do not suggest that these solutions will be easy to accomplish, particularly in a global context where fat bodies have been problematized for decades. However, solving the problem of fatphobia is achievable if we are willing to exert the political will and direct the resources necessary to do so.

Further reading

Farrell, A.E. (2011) *Fat Shame: Stigma and the Fat Body in American Culture.* New York, NY: New York University Press.

Greenhalgh, S. (2015) *Fat-Talk Nation: The Human Costs of America's War on Fat.* Ithaca, NY: Cornell University Press.

Hunger, J.M., Smith, J.P., and Tomiyama, A.J. (2020) An evidence-based rationale for adopting weight-inclusive health policy. *Social Issues and Policy Review*, 14(1): 73–107. Available at: https://doi.org/10.1111/sipr.12062

Medvedyuk, S., Ali, A., and Raphael, D. (2017) Ideology, obesity and the social determinants of health: a critical analysis of the obesity and health relationship. *Critical Public Health*, 28(5): 573–85. Available at: https://doi.org/10.1080/09581596.2017.1356910

O'Hara, L. and Taylor, J. (2018) What's wrong with the "war on obesity?" A narrative review of the weight-centered health paradigm and development of the 3C framework to build critical competency for a paradigm shift. *SAGE Open*, 18(2). Available at: https://doi.org/10.1177/2158244018772888

Oliver, J.E. (2006) *Fat Politics: The Real Story behind America's Obesity Epidemic.* Oxford: Oxford University Press.

Pomeranz, J.L. (2008) A historical analysis of public health, the law, and stigmatized social groups: the need for both obesity and weight bias legislation. *Obesity*, 16(S2): S93-103. Available at: https://doi.org/10.1038/oby.2008.452

Puhl, R.M. and Heuer, C.A. (2009) The stigma of obesity: a review and update. *Obesity*, 17: 941–6. Available at: https://doi.org/10.1038/oby.2008.636

Stoll, L.C. (2019) Fat is a social justice issue, too. *Humanity & Society*, 43(4): 421–41. Available at: https://doi.org/10.1177/0160597619832051

Von Liebenstein, S. (2021) Fatness, discrimination and law: an international perspective. In C. Pausé and S.R. Taylor (eds) *The Routledge International Handbook of Fat Studies.* New York, NY: Routledge, pp 132–49.

FIVE

Opioid abuse and evidence-based practices for a global epidemic

Andrea N. Hunt

The problem

Opium originated in lower Mesopotamia in 3,400 BC and was used in many regions of the world throughout history before making its way to the US. It was not until the 1860s that opium-based drugs, such as morphine, were used by Civil War doctors to treat the pain of wounded soldiers. The Bayer Company later introduced heroin as a cough suppressant and an alternative to morphine, with the US government placing restrictions in the 1910s–1920s that outlawed heroin and required a prescription for opioids. The Controlled Substance Act was passed in the 1970s, which created five different groupings, or schedules, for all substances based on their medical use, potential for abuse, and safety.

Opioids are a class of drugs used to treat pain and include both prescription medications (for example, OxyContin, hydrocodone, morphine, and fentanyl) and heroin. Misuse or abuse of opioids can lead to an addiction, which is clinically referred to as opioid use disorder. The opioid crisis began in the 1990s with the development and increased prescription of OxyContin to treat pain. US-based drug manufacturer Purdue Pharma assured that patients would not develop an opioid use disorder and pharmaceutical sales skyrocketed, with aggressive marketing strategies and plans to expand sales globally. That decade ended with a rising number of fatal overdoses directly related to the use of prescription opioids.

While efforts focused on the global seizure of pharmaceutical opioids, the unattended effect was rising global opium production, which resulted in an increase in heroin with low cost and high availability. By 2010, the second wave of opioid abuse hit the US, with prescription opioids still being misused, but this time, the overdose deaths were primarily due to heroin. The third and current wave began in 2013, with continued abuse of prescription opioids and heroin, but with an increased number of overdose deaths involving synthetic opioids. In North America, fentanyl has led to countless deaths. Pharmaceutical fentanyl is approved for treating severe cancer pain and is

50 to 100 times stronger than morphine. The fatal overdoses rarely involve pharmaceutical fentanyl, but illicitly manufactured fentanyl. In other parts of the world, Tramadol (another synthetic opioid) has led to an increase in overdoses.

While much of the attention around the opioid epidemic has focused on the US, other countries are not immune to its devastation, and many of these countries have led the way in exploring different treatment approaches. Pharmacotherapy is the most common treatment method used today. However, treatment for opioid use disorder is often fragmented, and this creates inequities in health and mental health access and outcomes. With this in mind, there is growing attention globally around the need for more physician education on pain management, alternatives to prescription drugs for the treatment of pain, the use of harm reduction methods, increased psychosocial treatment, and more research on the combined effectiveness of pharmacotherapeutic and psychosocial treatments.

Research evidence

The Centers for Disease Control and Prevention (CDC, 2021) has called the current levels of opioid abuse an epidemic, and the National Institute on Drug Abuse (2021) agrees that we are in a crisis. The World Health Organization (WHO, 2021) and the United Nations Office on Drugs and Crimes (UNODC, 2021) have both cited this as a global epidemic. Despite this recognition and awareness, recent data on the extent of opioid-related deaths across the world is scarce. The WHO (2021) provides some global estimates, finding that 115,000 people died of an opioid overdose in 2017. Most of the available data focuses on the US since it has been at the center of this epidemic since the 1990s. The WHO reports that fatal opioid overdoses in the US increased by 120 per cent between 2010 and 2018, and two thirds of the fatal opioid-related overdoses in 2018 involved fentanyl. According to the CDC, there were 50,000 opioid-related deaths in the US in 2019. With its proximity to the US, Canada also saw an increase in opioid abuse and opioid-related deaths related to fentanyl during this same time. The Canadian Public Health Association (2016) issued a position statement in 2016 acknowledging that existing approaches failed to reduce the number of overdoses and called for the Canadian government to do more to address the growing epidemic.

The UNODC (2021) "World drug report" highlighted the continued high levels of heroin and fentanyl use in the US and Canada. In other parts of the world, such as Southwest Asia (Afghanistan, Iran, and Pakistan), it is estimated that 6.8 million people used opioids in 2019. In Pakistan and India, it is heroin abuse, while in Afghanistan and Iran, opium is being abused. Iran also saw an increase in the use of the synthetic opioid Tramadol, with estimates ranging from 3.7 to 6 per cent of men and 0.1 to 3.3 per cent of women using the drug in 2019 for nonmedical reasons. There are no recent data for countries in East and Southeast Asia, but UNODC suggests that opioid use in these areas seems to have declined since 2010.

Heroin use is still common in many countries in Africa, but there is an increasing concern about the use of Tramadol in West, Central, and North Africa. Data from Nigeria suggest that 6 per cent of men and 3.3 per cent of women were estimated to have used opioids in 2017, which mainly consisted of Tramadol, along with lower uses of codeine and morphine. In North Africa, Tramadol has also been a major issue in Egypt, where it is estimated that 3 per cent of the adult population and 1.4 per cent of secondary students abused it in 2016. In other North African countries, school surveys show a different pattern, with heroin abused by adolescents in Algeria and Morocco, and buprenorphine used in Tunisia.

Data from the 2019 Australian Institute of Health and Welfare National Drug Strategy and Household Survey (Australian Institute of Health and Welfare, 2020) found a decrease in opioid use from 3.6 per cent of the population aged 14 and older in 2016 to 2.7 per cent in 2019. Codeine was the most commonly abused drug in 2016 and 2019, and was reclassified in 2018 as a schedule 4 drug in Australia, which made it more difficult to obtain. While the overall use of opioids declined, there was an increase in Tramadol and oxycodone abuse.

Recommendations and solutions

The overall efforts to reduce opioid abuse fall into one of three categories: demand reduction, supply reduction, and harm reduction. These approaches differ globally based on national policies toward opioid abuse, for example, whether it is criminalized or seen as a public health issue, which may vary for prescription opioids versus heroin (and who we think are using these drugs). While opioid abuse may sometimes be seen as an individual-level problem, understanding it as a societal issue is key to the implementation of demand, supply, and harm reduction practices.

Reducing the demand for opioids

To reduce demand for prescription opioids calls for physician education and alternative treatments for pain management. The most important skills for physicians in addressing and managing opioid abuse are to learn more effective ways to monitor and assess for risk. Physicians need ongoing education and professional development in opioid risk management, and that includes the increasing use of physical therapy, acupuncture, mind–body therapies, and chiropractic care for pain. While medication is the most common treatment method for chronic pain, primary care doctors often do not have training in this area. Recently, practice guidelines were developed to assist primary care doctors, but their implementation can vary by country and be affected by insurance practices, professional associations, and/or local codes. This is further complicated by the lobbying power and aggressive sales tactics of pharmaceutical companies, such as US-based Purdue Pharma, maker of OxyContin, which is known for its role in the opioid epidemic. This is a topic of concern for many medical professionals, scientists, and pain experts, who are collaborating through the World Congress on Regional Anesthesia and Pain Medicine to develop global strategies for acute and chronic pain management that reduce the demand for opioids and increase the availability of alternative treatments for pain, such as occupational therapy, physical therapy, and acupuncture.

Reducing the supply of opioids

The US Institute for Behavior and Health suggests that supply reduction works hand in hand with demand reduction and that using these approaches simultaneously maximizes the ability to effect change in the global opioid epidemic. Supply reduction can be seen in efforts to: reduce the amount of controlled opioid substances (that is, fentanyl, hydrocodone, hydromorphone, oxycodone, and oxymorphone) that can be manufactured; increase the criminal prosecution of doctors who overprescribe or unnecessarily prescribe opioids; destroy opium poppy crops and introduce alternative crops as a way to sustain economic livelihood; interrupt drug-trafficking routes; and increase punishments for the illegal sale of opioids.

These efforts and their effectiveness vary globally. For example, the destruction of opium poppy crops is a strategy that has been used in such places as Afghanistan, Laos, Myanmar, and Mexico, which are some of the countries with the most poppy fields. Since the 1940s, the US received most of its heroin from Mexico, and in 2017, their poppy crops reached an all-time high. Laos and Myanmar are considered part of the Golden Triangle, and they have had historically high rates of opium crops. Poppy crops in these areas have declined over time, and Afghanistan now accounts for about 80 per cent of crop production. These crops are in high demand because unripe opium poppy seeds are used in a variety of drugs, including opium, morphine, codeine, and heroin. Crop destruction is complicated in many countries because opium poppy crops are widespread, especially in rural or remote areas, where there are varying interests and stakeholders involved in the cultivation of these crops, such as farmers, traffickers, insurgents, local governments, international coalitions, and intergovernmental organizations (for example, the United Nations). These competing interests rest on who is profiting and at what rate, while other interests center on who is affected by the mass production of opium poppy. What is needed are alternatives for economic livelihood that are sustainable. This means that these alternatives must be supported by the state with equitable development resources, such as land titles, microcredit, stable infrastructures, access to agricultural processing plants, and trade and export opportunities.

As cryptomarkets have emerged, where buyers and sellers engage in online drug-related transactions on the darknet with more anonymity, intergovernmental cooperation is needed to manage the digital drug trade and develop policies to target the dark web. An important first step in this process occurred when the Federal Bureau of Investigation (FBI) and Europol shut down the Silk Road, which was the world's first major drug cryptomarket. However, the European Monitoring Centre for Drugs and Drug Addiction (EMCDDA) and Europol suggest that law enforcement has only been able to temporarily disrupt darknet markets, with new virtual markets establishing much quicker than previous land-based drug-trafficking routes. In 2019, Interpol held its second Global Conference on Illicit Drugs, with 400 experts from 100 countries meeting to discuss new ways of supply reduction that require information sharing and collaboration in an ever-increasing transnational and virtual drug network.

The use of harm reduction strategies

Harm reduction methods (that is, medication-assisted treatment or pharmacotherapy), the most common evidence-based treatment options for opioid abuse, need to be expanded. Methadone, buprenorphine, extended-release naltrexone, and Suboxone (a combination of buprenorphine and naloxone) are the current medications prescribed for treatment. Pharmacotherapy is used in inpatient, residential, and outpatient treatment settings, and can also be effective in primary care/office-based settings (Gordon and Oliva, 2018). Pharmacotherapeutic treatment in primary care/office-based settings includes the initial prescription, monitoring for stabilization, and ongoing maintenance. There are also additional psychosocial supports in primary care/office-based settings, but this is not universal.

Hospital emergency departments are an important point of access for many people, especially those without a primary care doctor. Emergency personnel are seeing a growing number of patients amid an overdose. More resources are needed for hospital emergency departments to increase pharmacotherapeutic treatment. Currently, buprenorphine induction programs allow patients a three-day prescription for buprenorphine to relieve withdrawal symptoms as a patient finds ongoing treatment. Care coordination is vital and includes referrals to primary care/office-based settings, community-based providers, and psychosocial supports. There is a growing body of research in this area, but more funding is needed to further research on the effectiveness of harm reduction care plans within hospital emergency departments. Funding agencies should prioritize research focused on expanding access to pharmacotherapy outside of traditional healthcare settings, which is particularly relevant for people in rural and remote areas, where access to healthcare is limited.

Increasing the efficacy of needle exchange programs by including other forms of therapy can be effective in reducing the number of people addicted and the health problems associated with opioid use. Needle and syringe exchange programs for opioid users is an important and effective harm reduction method that is used globally, and they are a potential way of also providing pharmacotherapy. These programs are effective in reducing the sharing of needles and syringes. The WHO, UNODC, and Joint United Nations Programme on HIV/AIDS (WHO, UNODC, and UNAIDS, 2009) recommend that exchange programs provide 200 sterile needles and syringes per person who injects psychoactive drugs per year as a way to reduce the potential transmission of HIV and hepatitis B and C. There is not a comprehensive list of countries with needle and syringe exchange programs because funding for these programs is not always stable, as governmental priorities change. Avert (n.d.)—a UK-based charitable organization focused on global information and HIV/AIDS education—reports that there were at least 179 countries with needle and syringe exchange programs in 2018.

Funding should be increased for low-threshold treatment programs, which do not require drug abstinence as a condition for assistance and may or may not include needle and syringe exchange. The focus is on removing barriers to treatment through targeted healthcare that reduces the long wait times for some outpatient treatment options and providing more affordable services. These programs also try to address the limited medication options for pharmacotherapy and the frequent urine testing that is often weekly for high-risk clients. This results in clients having earlier and more frequent contact with program staff.

Psychosocial treatment should be used in conjunction with pharmacotherapeutic treatment. It includes a needs assessment, counseling, family supports, and referrals to community services. Access to psychosocial treatment varies globally, and there is little research on evidence-based psychosocial interventions for improving outcomes for opioid abuse. There are promising results for using mindfulness-based relapse prevention (MBRP) with clients, increasing their self-awareness regarding their opioid abuse (Dugosh et al, 2016). The Recovery Community Center Office-Based Opioid Treatment (RCCOBOT) model is another effective approach that reduces barriers for pharmacotherapy and psychotherapy by using peer support specialists (Ashford et al, 2019). While individual counseling is often included in psychosocial treatment, there is little research on the comparative advantages of specific types of therapeutic approaches and very little research on group therapy for opioid use disorder. The National Institute of Health's (NIH's) Helping to End Addiction Long-term Initiative (n.d.) needs to continue to prioritize grant funding for research on treatment for opioid abuse and, specifically, to support studies that assess which psychosocial treatments are most effective for different patient populations and how those can be used in conjunction with pharmacotherapy.

References

Ashford, R.D., Brown, A.M., McDaniel, J., Neasbitt, J., Sobora, C., Riley, R., Weinstein, L., Laxton, A., Kunzelman, J., Kampman, K., and Curtis, B. (2019) Responding to the opioid and overdose crisis with innovative services: the Recovery Community Center Office-Based Opioid Treatment (RCC-OBOT) model. *Addictive Behavior*, 98: 1–8.

Australian Institute of Health and Welfare (2020) National Drug Strategy Household Survey 2019. Available at: https://www.aihw.gov.au/getmedia/77dbea6e-f071-495c-b71e-3a632237269d/aihw-phe-270.pdf.aspx?inline=true

Avert (n.d.) Available at: https://avert.info

Canadian Public Health Association (2016) The opioid crisis in Canada. Available at: www.cpha.ca/sites/default/files/uploads/policy/positionstatements/opioid-positionstatement-e.pdf

CDC (Centers for Disease Control and Prevention) (2021) Opioid data analysis and resources. Available at: www.cdc.gov/drugoverdose/data/analysis.html

Dugosh, K., Abraham, A., Seymour, B., McLoyd, K., Chalk, M., and Festinger, D. (2016) A systematic review on the use of psychosocial interventions in conjunction with medications for the treatment of opioid addiction. *Journal of Addiction Medicine*, 10(2): 91–101.

Gordon, A.J. and Oliva, E.M. (2018) Applying and advancing best practices in opioid use disorder and addiction treatment: introduction to the special issue on implementation science and quality improvement scholarship. *Substance Abuse*, 39(2): 125–8. Available at: https://doi.org/10.1080/08897077.2018.1518082

National Institute on Drug Abuse (2021) Opioid overdose crisis. Available at: www.drugabuse.gov/drug-topics/opioids/opioid-overdose-crisis

National Institutes of Health Initiative (n.d.) The helping to end addiction long-term® initiative. Available at: https://heal.nih.gov/

UNODC (United Nations Office on Drugs and Crime) (2021) World drug report, drug market trends: Cannabis, opioids. Available at: www.unodc.org/res/wdr2021/field/WDR21_Booklet_3.pdf

WHO (World Health Organization) (2021) Opioid overdose. Available at: www.who.int/news-room/fact-sheets/detail/opioid-overdose

WHO, UNODC (United Nations Office on Drugs and Crime), and UNAIDS (Joint United Nations Programme on HIV/AIDS) (2009) Technical guide for countries to set targets for universal access to HIV prevention, treatment and care for injecting drug users. Available at: www.unaids.org/sites/default/files/sub_landing/idu_target_setting_guide_en.pdf

Further reading

Ho, J. (2019) The contemporary American drug overdose epidemic in international perspective. *Population and Development Review*, 45(1): 7–40.

Imani, S., Vahid, M.K.A., Gharraee, B., Noroozi, A., Habibi, M., and Bowen, S. (2015) Effectiveness of mindfulness-based group therapy compared to the usual opioid dependence treatment. *Iran Journal of Psychiatry*, 10(3): 175–84.

Krausz, R.M., Westenberg, J.N., and Ziafat, K. (2021) The opioid overdose crisis as a global health challenge. *Current Opinion in Psychiatry*, 34(4): 405–12.

SIX

Water justice as social policy: tackling the global challenges to water and sanitation access

Marie Carmen Shingne and Stephen P. Gasteyer

The problem

Globally, an estimated one in four people still lack access to safe drinking water and nearly half of the global population—about 3.6 billion people—lack access to safe sanitation services (WHO, 2019). These statistics have shifted drastically over the years, depending on how access and safety are defined. Back in 2015, when safe water and sanitation were synonymous with improved sources—meaning likely to be protected from outside contamination through construction or intervention—it was estimated that over 90 per cent of the world's population had access to safe water and only 2.4 billion people lacked access to safe sanitation services (UNICEF and WHO, 2015). The discrepancies between these two sets of statistics underpin the significant challenges still faced in measuring and increasing access to safe drinking water and sanitation services around the world. The ever-changing definitions of what constitutes safe water and sanitation have made it difficult to collect consistent statistical data on the situation, with access either over- or underestimated, depending on the definition. Furthermore, due to a focus on technological efforts, negative shifts in access may well be indications of backsliding, for example, when infrastructure breaks or loses efficacy. In combination with a growing body of scholarly and gray literature highlighting the systemic nature of inequalities influencing water poverty (see UNICEF and WHO, 2015; Anand, 2017; DigDeep, 2019; TMI, 2019), there is a need for a more holistic and sustained shift in how safe water and sanitation are defined, in how data are collected, and toward policy- rather than technology-focused efforts.

Research evidence

International monitoring initiatives related to water and sanitation date back to the 1930s. The first questionnaires were administered by the League of Nations Health Organization, the predecessor of the World Health Organization (WHO) (Bartram et al, 2014; Herrera, 2019). Data from these early questionnaires were often incomplete, varied drastically across years, and were not independently verified. The United Nations (UN) has made multiple attempts to improve on these early questionnaires, with its most recent efforts being Target 7C of the Millennium Development Goals (MDGs) in 2000 and Sustainable Development Goal (SDG) 6, adopted along with 16 other SDGs in 2015.

Despite nearly a century of efforts, the global community continues to struggle in providing universal access to potable water and sanitation. Scholars attribute much of this struggle to the limitations of measurement efforts and too frequent reliance on a one-size-fits-all technocratic approach. Under SDG 6, the best water source is a "safely managed" source, defined as an improved source, on premises, available as needed, and free from fecal and priority chemical contamination. In many rural communities, boreholes and wells are the best options for water access, but to be on premises would mean that each household would need to have its own well. More wells would lower the water table and therefore access (Adams and Smiley, 2018). Instead, community wells could achieve equitable access much better, especially with greater focus on the funding and maintenance of existing wells (policies), rather than on providing every household with a well (technology). Similarly, in highly populated urban and peri-urban settings, especially informal ones, community-managed public toilets and washing facilities are often the most appropriate solution, despite going against currently accepted definitions of safely managed water (Satterthwaite, 2016).

Even the existence of a borehole or well as constituting water access misrepresents the lived reality (Adams and Smiley, 2018). Seasonal cycles between drought and rain greatly influence the water level of these sources. Peri-urban and urban communities may similarly face availability issues, but theirs are influenced by shutoffs, rationing, and insufficient pressure within the pipes. In both cases, a water source exists in the vicinity, but neither is necessarily a *secure* (that is, reliable) source. Peri-urban neighborhoods in Dar es Salaam, Tanzania, have existing water systems supplied by the municipal utility company, but residents experience frequent water cutoffs because of the low supply and obsolete and degraded conveyance infrastructure, and must rely on alternative water supplies (Ngasala et al, 2019). These alternative supplies are plagued by both local and non-local sewage contamination, leading to repeated cholera outbreaks in the community. Installed in the 1970s, the pipes for the Mumbai neighborhood of Premnagar have long since fallen into disrepair—rusting, leaking, and running dry (Anand, 2011, 2012, 2017). In the Palestinian communities of Abud and Dura, pipes convey water into homes, but frequent cutoffs render those piped water systems nonfunctional (Abu Madi et al, 2017). Similarly in low-income communities across the US, the infrastructure theoretically exists for water and sanitation access, but these systems do not deliver consistent and reliable water and sanitation, forcing residents to buy expensive bottled water (DigDeep, 2019).

There are also political forces at work, hidden by the technocratic focus. Traditionally, human water systems have been viewed from a water scarcity lens (Gain et al, 2016), with a focus on the physical water and what technology is needed to access it (Roy and Pramanick, 2019). This view fails to recognize that unequitable distribution of water resources is fueled by economic disparity, poor governance, and historical sociopolitical dynamics, including colonial relations (Gain et al, 2016; Shah, 2016; Adams and Smiley, 2018). Water and sanitation management and project implementation are commonly overseen by elected officials and, therefore, greatly determined and influenced by partisan goals and beliefs (Anand, 2011, 2012; Herrera, 2019). Neighborhoods are often rewarded for electoral support with water access or, alternatively, face corruption. For Palestine, the struggle for access to water in the West Bank is intrinsically tied to the inequities associated with Israeli settler colonialism. This includes the history of Palestinian displacement, which started in the 1930s, and the rules intended to create Israeli-Jewish hegemony over the water system (*Al Haq*, 2013). The water problems faced by the peri-urban communities of Dar es Salaam are connected to a history of rural–urban migration associated with the economic policy that allowed conditions in rural communities to deteriorate, as well as the inability of municipal officials to serve the needs of an African mega-city (Duda et al, 2018). City officials view the Premnagar residents in Mumbai with distrust because of their outsider status—Muslim (non-Hindu) migrants from the northern Indian state of Uttar Pradesh (Anand, 2012). This distrust manifests in a lack of water service provision and system maintenance.

Recommendations and solutions

To achieve truly equitable water access, historical inequalities must be addressed within the political sphere and financial efforts must be made to ensure continued access after the initial investment in technology. The recommendations we outline in the following take these concerns to heart, while also building off the existing structure of SDG 6, in particular, Targets 6.1, 6.2, 6.5, and 6b. First, improvements must be made to the terminology encompassed in Targets 6.1 and 6.2, with greater clarity and specificity as to what it means to aim for universal and equitable access to safe, affordable drinking water and adequate and equitable sanitation for all. We also make recommendations about how to better implement water management strategies at *all* levels, as designated by Target 6.5, and particularly how to better integrate local communities in solutions, as per Target 6b.

Extend definition to include water security

Our first recommendation is that the definition of water access needs to be extended to include *security*: "[w]ater security is rooted not only in the physical availability of freshwater resources relative to water demand, but also on social and economic factors (e.g. sound water planning and management approaches, institutional capacity to provide water services, sustainable economic policies)" (Gain et al, 2016: 124015). Any new projects and efforts need to move away from a focus on the *existence* of "improved" or "safely managed" water sources and actively include contextual measures of contamination, reliability, affordability, and management. These variables are drawn from the human right to water, officially recognized by the UN in 2010, defined as: "the right of everyone to sufficient, safe, acceptable, physically accessible and affordable water for personal and domestic uses" (UN, 2002: 2; see also UN, 2010).

Improve data-collection methods

Deepening the definition of water access will do no good if the mechanisms to measure this deepened definition are not present. Collecting accurate information is essential for ensuring the success of programs, as well as access to funding, as recent overestimations of success—as in the case of MDG 7C—may lead to the reallocation of funding away from the water sector even as the situation remains unresolved (Martínez-Santos, 2017). Therefore, we recommend that data are collected on five essential characteristics of water source and access, again drawing from the human right to water: the (1) type and (2) accessibility of the source; and the (3) availability, (4) affordability, and (5) safety of the water (Gain et al, 2016; Adams and Smiley, 2018).

Furthermore, we recommend a shift away from relying solely on household surveys and toward a more in-depth case-study approach (Lockwood et al, 2010; Bartram et al, 2014). Household surveys face several key shortcomings, including interpretation error in answering questions and biased responses like courtesy (what the interviewer wants to hear) and social desirability (framing participants in a favorable light) (Martínez-Santos, 2017). The household level also misses finer-tuned detail, as when household size may play a role in water access. Finally, the statistical data of surveys only provide a "static snapshot" of the reality, providing "little indication of the functionality of physical systems, much less the quality or quantity of the service being provided" (Lockwood et al, 2010: 3). Case studies can better capture more nuanced definitions of water access, capturing water source "portfolios" rather than only the most common or visible source, and considering cyclical changes like access during dry versus monsoon seasons. We would encourage the reader to explore the DigDeep (2019) report, which took a case-study approach to six communities lacking access to water in the US.

Pair technocratic approaches with political and economic changes

Integrated approaches spanning from local to broad systems

One noted weakness of existing efforts is their project-based focus, which sidesteps governmental involvement and lacks scalability (Lockwood et al, 2010). Local-, household-, and community-level efforts are needed to put infrastructure and resources into place, but these alone are not enough. To ensure sustainability and longevity of service, these localized efforts must be fit into a larger systemic effort at the intermediate level, defined as at the district, municipal, or regional scale. Maintaining the access achieved through infrastructural updates requires a "thorough understanding of the full life-cycle costs and institutional support needs" of a water and sanitation system (Lockwood et al, 2010: 9). It also requires recognition that water systems do not exist in isolation, but rather as part of a greater political, economic, and ecological system (Agenda for Change, 2020).

To achieve this more systemic engagement, we recommend taking a service delivery approach, shifting from focusing on individual projects to instead focusing on the services as a whole. In other words, taking a holistic approach from developing a project and installing the initial technology to the longer-term policy, institutional, and financial frameworks that will allow for long-term access, taking both soft (skills, behaviors, norms, practices, and so on) and hard (technologies, finances, and so on) factors into account. Starting in 2006, the group Water for People worked with a local Bolivian development organization, the Instituto de Capacitación para el Desarrollo (INCADE), to develop water-supply projects in the San Pedro municipality. By 2011, the municipality had established and earmarked funding for a municipal Water, Sanitation, and Hygiene (WASH) office to manage all water and sanitation work in the municipality. Water for People noted that key lessons learned were the need to: (1) shift away from project-based funding; (2) focus on outcomes (district-wide services) rather than outputs (the number of people served by new infrastructure); and (3) adjust their organizational planning processes to better align with the planning cycles of the local government (Agenda for Change, 2020).

There are other examples from around the world, where academic institutions, community groups, and nonprofit organizations are identifying contextually appropriate methods and implementing them in collaboration with local governments and systems. For example, there is a pilot project by the University of California, Los Angeles, called the Salinas Valley Distributed Water Treatment Project. This takes a decentralized, community approach, with the goal of providing safe and affordable drinking water to Central Valley residents in low-income housing developments by using distributed reverse osmosis membrane treatment (DigDeep, 2019). In Palestine, in lieu of groundwater and reliable delivery of Israeli National Water Carrier water, communities have worked to implement water-catchment systems to harvest runoff in order to augment supply for irrigation of household gardens and livestock (which are important for food security and livelihoods). There have also been increasing efforts to implement village-level wastewater treatment and reuse facilities that can augment water supplies. Likewise, efforts are under way in peri-urban Dar es Salaam to improve sanitation management in an effort to mitigate water-quality contamination and improve public health.

Local actors in positions of power

Part of this integrated approach is providing local communities with greater autonomy. Many local communities and community groups already know what they need; they just need those in power to listen to them or to hold the power themselves. The Community Water Center (CWC) is a grassroots environmental justice organization already providing short-term assistance and advocating for larger and longer-term policy-based changes in the Central Valley of California (DigDeep, 2019). Part of its work has included helping local communities to shake up their water boards and elect local residents in place of career politicians. The CWC has helped provide water deliveries, point-of-use filters, and private well testing. It has also mobilized local communities to demand that policymakers be more responsive to their needs, replacing career politicians on the water boards with local residents and pushing Sacramento lawmakers to pass statewide legislation affirming the human right to water, creating mechanisms for the mandatory consolidation of water systems, and freeing up state emergency funding for water deliveries.

Drawing on the strength of community members could prove essential in other rural communities around the world. In the outlying Dar es Salaam neighborhoods in Tanzania, understanding the significant capacity of women to balance multiple water sources and building on that knowledge could provide key insights into successfully addressing household water scarcity and quality in these communities.

More holistic funding

If it is accepted that solutions must fully engage local communities, current external funding systems must be reconsidered. Donors must "listen to, work with, and support local governments and civil society organizations to develop locally appropriate solutions, including co-production. This also has to go beyond supporting a few innovative 'community' initiatives to developing the financial and institutional means to support this at scale" (Satterthwaite, 2016: 116–17). In other words, funding sources must work with local actors to pair available funding with needed long-term solutions, not only individual initiatives. This includes funding previously disregarded projects and communities, including shared and community toilets and wells, as well as the representative organizations of slum and shack residents, rather than only being willing to allocate funding to individual residents themselves.

Conclusion

The concern over access to potable water will only intensify as the effects of global climate change become more widespread. In many of the examples we have highlighted earlier, climate change is exacerbating water hardship. Wells in California's Central Valley and in the *colonias* along the Texas–Mexico border have dried up due to climate-change-induced droughts, causing hardship both in the need to import water and due to the contamination of wells and the associated health risks. Water shutoffs in Dar es Salaam, Abud, and Dura have been prolonged due to declines in precipitation because of climate change. As water becomes an ever-scarcer resource, political systems must adapt in ways that do not repeat and perpetuate the historical and systemic infrastructural violence outlined earlier.

References

Abu Madi, M., Gasteyer, S.P., and Ghadeer A.A. (2017) *The Social Implications of Prepaid Water Meters and Intermittent Water Supply in the West Bank, Palestine: Technical Report*. Birzeit, Palestine: Birzeit University.

Adams, E.A. and Smiley, S.L. (2018) Urban–rural water access inequalities in Malawi: implications for monitoring the Sustainable Development Goals. *Natural Resources Forum*, 42(4): 217–26.

Agenda for Change (2020) Strengthening water, sanitation, and hygiene systems: concepts, examples, and experiences. February. Available at: https://washagendaforchange.org/wp-content/uploads/2020/04/20200227_agenda_for_change_systems_strengthening_experiences_final.pdf

Al Haq (2013) Water for one people only: discriminatory access and "water-apartheid" in the OPT. *Al Haq*, July 31. Available at: www.alhaq.org/publications/8073.html

Anand, N. (2011) PRESSURE: the PoliTechnics of water supply in Mumbai. *Cultural Anthropology*, 26(4): 542–64.

Anand, N. (2012) Municipal disconnect: on abject water and its urban infrastructures. *Ethnography*, 13(4): 487–509.

Anand, N. (2017) *Hydraulic City: Water & the Infrastructures of Citizenship in Mumbai*. Durham, NC: Duke University Press.

Bartram, J., Brocklehurst, C., Fisher, M.B., Luyendijk, R., Hossain, R., Wardlaw, T., and Gordon, B. (2014) Global monitoring of water supply and sanitation: history, methods and future challenges. *International Journal of Environmental Research and Public Health*, 11(8): 8137–65.

DigDeep (2019) Closing the water access gap in the United States: a national action plan. Report by DigDeep and the U.S. Water Alliance. Available at: www.digdeep.org/close-the-water-gap/

Duda, I., Fasse, A., and Grote, U. (2018) Drivers of rural–urban migration and impact on food security in rural Tanzania. *Food Security*, 10: 785–98.

Gain, A.K., Giupponi, C., and Wada Y. (2016) Measuring global water security towards Sustainable Development Goals. *Environmental Research Letter*, 11: 124015.

Herrera, V. (2019) Reconciling global aspirations and local realities: challenges facing the Sustainable Development Goals for water and sanitation. *World Development*, 118: 106–17.

Lockwood, H., Smits, S., Schouten, T., and Moriarty, P. (2010) Providing sustainable water services at scale. International Symposium on Rural Water Services, April 13–15. Available at: www.ircwash.org/sites/default/files/Lockwood-2010-Providing.pdf

Martínez-Santos, P. (2017) Does 91% of the world's population really have "sustainable access to safe drinking water"? *International Journal of Water Resources Development*, 33(4): 514–33. Available at: https://doi.org/10.1080/07900627.2017.1298517

Ngasala T.M., Gasteyer, S.P., Masten, S.J., and Phanikumar, M.S. (2019) Linking cross contamination of domestic water with storage practices at the point of use in urban areas of Dar es Salaam, Tanzania. *Journal of Environmental Engineering*, 145(5): 04019017. Available at: https://doi.org/10.1061/(ASCE)EE.1943-7870.0001516

Roy, A. and Pramanick, K. (2019) Analysing progress of Sustainable Development Goal 6 in India: past, present, and future. *Journal of Environmental Management*, 232: 1049–65.

Satterthwaite, D. (2016) Missing the Millennium Development Goal targets for water and sanitation in urban areas. *Environment & Urbanization*, 28(1): 99–118.

Shah, T. (2016) Increasing water security: the key to implementing the Sustainable Development Goals. Global Water Partnership (GWP) TEC Background Papers, No. 22.

TMI (Thurgood Marshall Institute) (2019) Water/color: a study of race & the water affordability crisis in America's cities. Available at: www.naacpldf.org/wp-content/uploads/Water_Report_Executive-Summary_5_21_19_FINAL-V2.pdf

UN (United Nations) (2002) General comment no. 15. The right to water. UN Committee on Economic, Social and Cultural Rights, November.

UN (2010) Resolution A/RES/64/292. United Nations General Assembly, July.

UNICEF (United Nations Children's Fund) and WHO (World Health Organization) (2015) Progress on sanitation and drinking water—2015 update and MDG assessment. Available at: https://www.who.int/publications/i/item/9789241509145

UNICEF and WHO (2019) *Progress on Household Drinking Water, Sanitation and Hygiene 2000–2017. Special Focus on Inequalities.* New York, NY: UNICEF.

WHO (World Health Organization) (2019) 1 in 3 people globally do not have access to safe drinking water—UNICEF, WHO. *World Health Organization News*, June 18. Available at: www.who.int/news/item/18-06-2019-1-in-3-people-globally-do-not-have-access-to-safe-drinking-water-unicef-who

Further reading

Flowers, C.C. and Stevenson, B. (2020) *Waste: One Woman's Fight against America's Dirty Secret.* New York, NY: The New Press.

Swyngedouw, E. (2004) *Social Power and the Urbanization of Water: Flows of Power.* New York, NY: Oxford University Press.

Winkler, I.T. (2014) *The Human Right to Water: Significance, Legal Status and Implications for Water Allocation.* Portland, OR: Hart Publishing.

SEVEN

COVID-19 vaccine inequity

Seow Ting Lee

The problem

In a global pandemic, a critical challenge is ensuring widespread access to vaccines to achieve needed levels of population immunity. With the first vaccine rollout in early 2021, 15 COVID-19 vaccines are currently in use worldwide, with Oxford-AstraZeneca and Pfizer-BioNTech doses being the most prevalent. By August 2021, of the 5.5 billion COVID-19 vaccine doses administered globally, 80 per cent had gone to high- or upper-middle-income countries. Only 0.2 per cent had been delivered to low-income countries. In high-income nations, one in four people had been vaccinated, a ratio that plummets to one in 500 in poorer countries.

Despite international efforts to address vaccine access, most notably, through the creation of COVID-19 Vaccines Global Access (COVAX), a global vaccine-sharing program, low- and middle-income countries are struggling to procure vaccines in a market cornered by rich nations, who are willing to pay premiums to hoard vaccines while slow-walking financial pledges that COVAX needed to purchase vaccines from manufacturers.

Vaccine inequity is not only a moral problem, but also economically and epidemiologically self-defeating. It affects the entire global community, fueling the rise of new, vaccine-resistant variants and dragging down the economies of rich and poor nations—and vaccinated and unvaccinated populations—alike. Data from the US National Bureau of Economic Research show that due to the interconnectedness of the global economy, COVID-19 outcomes for the entire global economy are highly dependent on poorer countries' populations getting vaccinated. Richer economies will still bear 49 per cent of the global costs of the pandemic, even if their own populations are entirely inoculated. There is another practical reason to distribute vaccines equitably and quickly. The unvaccinated serve as "variant factories" that create more mutations that accelerate and prolong the pandemic. As long as the virus continues to spread, it will breach borders and impede global recovery. No part of the world is safe if the pandemic rages on elsewhere, potentially spawning more dangerous, vaccine-resistant variants.

On May 24, 2021, World Health Organization (WHO) Director-General Tedros Adhanom Ghebreyesus slammed wealthy countries for facilitating a "scandalous inequity" in COVID-19 vaccines that is prolonging the COVID-19 pandemic: "There is no diplomatic way to say it: a small group of countries that make and buy the majority of the world's vaccines control the fate of the rest of the world" (World Health Organization, 2021a). According to United Nations Secretary-General Antonio Guterres, ten countries alone account for nearly 80 per cent of the vaccine doses administered globally (United Nations, 2021a). In July 2021, the WHO condemned rich countries and vaccine manufacturers for prioritizing their booster (third) shots even as poorer nations struggled to give the first and second doses to their healthcare workers and at-risk populations (World Health Organization, 2021b).

Research evidence

Months before the first COVID-19 vaccine was approved, vaccine nationalism emerged as wealthy nations began stockpiling, via preorders, billions of advance doses for their citizens. By the end of 2020, Canada had purchased 338 million doses, enough to vaccinate its population four times over. The UK purchased three times what it needed to inoculate its citizens. By February 2021, 56 per cent of COVID-19 vaccines had been purchased by high-income nations, who represent 16 per cent of the global population—highlighting the disparities laid bare by COVID-19 that continue to compromise our collective ability to control the pandemic.

On May 27, 2021, the WHO Strategic Advisory Group of Experts on Immunization noted that the "[i]nequity is decreasing, but high-income nations have administered 69 times more doses per inhabitant than low-income countries" (Burki, 2021). In June 2021, six months after the first COVID-19 vaccine rollout, high-income nations had administered almost 44 per cent of the world's doses, compared to 0.4 per cent in low-income countries. Of the 1.5 billion doses of COVID-19 vaccine administered globally, more than 330 million have been administered in the US, where more than 60 per cent of its population have received at least one dose. "Increasingly, we see a two-track pandemic," said the WHO's Tedros, who added that "the most frustrating thing about this statistic is that it hasn't changed in months" (World Health Organization, 2021a).

Even without the complexities posed by new COVID-19 variants, the inequitable access to vaccines is problematic. According to the Duke Global Innovation Center Launch and Scale Speedometer, which monitors COVID-19 vaccine purchases by countries, at the current rate of vaccine access, there will not be enough vaccine doses to cover the world's population until at least 2023 (Duke University, no date). The inequity is even more pronounced when looking at the share of who could be vaccinated. While enough vaccine doses have been purchased to cover more than 80 per cent of the world's adult population, high-income nations own enough doses to vaccinate more than twice their populations, while lower- and middle-income countries can cover only one third of their populations. More troubling, there is a direct relationship between wealth and vaccine access. UN data from April 2021 reported that the number of doses administered in low-income countries covered only 0.2 per cent of their populations, compared to 16.7 per cent in middle-income countries and 48.7 per cent in high-income nations. The persistent vaccine inequity has prompted the WHO to call for a moratorium on booster shots to enable every country to vaccinate at least 40 per cent of their populations by the end of 2021.

In Africa, many countries, including Angola, Namibia, and Uganda, have been seeing sharp rises in COVID-19 cases and little progress in vaccination. Only 31.4 million doses have been administered in 50 African nations, which translates into a mere 2 per cent of the population receiving a single dose. Yet, in the UK, more than 40 million people—over 70 per cent of the adult population—have received at least one dose. Globally, the average is 24 per cent.

Experts have projected that 11 billion doses of vaccines are needed worldwide to slow the spread of the virus. By August 2021, COVAX has shipped only 245 million doses, mostly free to poor countries. Of the expected delivery of 1.9 billion doses in 2021, it anticipates a shortfall of 500 million doses.

Recommendations and solutions

Universal access to COVID-19 vaccines requires absolute commitment from all parties and coordinated global effort, focusing not only on infrastructure investment, technology and knowledge transfer, and a competent global regulatory system, but also moral leadership and a recalibration in nations' willingness to share based on principles of solidarity and equity.

Strengthening the COVAX framework

COVAX was created in 2020 as an international partnership led by the Coalition for Epidemic Preparedness Innovations, Gavi, the Vaccine Alliance, and the WHO. One of COVAX's main efforts focuses on purchasing COVID-19 vaccine doses in bulk, at a discount, for distribution to the world's most resource-strapped countries. Although it established a global purchasing and distribution pool, particularly for poorer nations that could not strike large prepurchase deals or manufacture their own vaccines, COVAX has struggled to deliver.

First, COVAX needs to add more vaccines to its arsenal. It should start by reducing its reliance on a limited pool of vaccines. Its two major suppliers are BioNTech and Moderna, who are selling their vaccines to COVAX at a discount. On paper, the framework seems to work: almost every country has signed up and COVAX began delivering vaccines on February 24, 2021, just two months after vaccinations started in Europe. However, supply issues soon emerged because the program is heavily reliant on the AstraZeneca vaccine and was challenged by delays in shipments from a key manufacturer, the Serum Institute of India, after the country halted exports due to a devastating outbreak in March 2021.

Second, instead of prioritizing vaccines as booster third shots to countries whose populations have relatively high coverage, vaccine manufacturers should channel their supplies to COVAX first to make more doses available to potential vaccine adopters. As new variants emerge, there is pressure to consider booster fourth shots, but COVAX needs as many doses as possible to dispense first and second shots in countries with low vaccine coverage.

Third, COVAX needs more financial resources to compete with high-income nations that cornered the market early on by striking purchase deals with vaccine makers. The problem, noted the WHO's Tedros, was "not getting vaccines out of COVAX"; rather, "The problem is getting them in" (United Nations, 2021b). Rich nations should channel more financial support to COVAX. Currently, COVAX prefers AstraZeneca because the vaccine is cheaper than messenger ribonucleic acid (mRNA) vaccines, some of which also require sub-zero transportation and storage arrangements—a challenge in poor countries, many of them in tropical climates. More financial support from high-income nations will also help COVAX expand its role in vaccine research and manufacturing by creating more vaccine production hubs in regions of distribution. Five hubs—all focused on mRNA vaccines—are being planned in Rwanda, Senegal, and South Africa. This approach would help COVAX reduce its reliance on purchases and expand its supply for faster delivery to more countries.

Fourth, more vaccine donations from high-income nations would help tremendously. A May 2021 report by the Independent Panel for Pandemic Preparedness and Response (IPPPR) projected that at their current rate of vaccination, many wealthy nations will have enough to donate 2 billion doses of vaccines by mid-2022, without compromising their own vaccination goals of inoculating at least 80 per cent of their populations older than 12 years. Donated doses, many of which would expire eventually, could help countries in need now. However, many high-income nations are hesitant, being concerned that excess doses would be needed after all due to uncertainties surrounding variants, possible new outbreaks, and the need for booster doses. Only two countries—Norway and New Zealand—have given back to COVAX the vaccines they were eligible to receive through the program.

Although a number of countries have expressed a readiness to share their unused vaccines, most of the donations have yet to occur.

Addressing a leadership vacuum at the global level

COVID-19 has not only underlined the long-term neglect of global public health, but also highlighted a leadership vacuum on the world stage. As countries struggle to contain the virus, reactive strategies, such as early stockpiling by the US and other high-income nations, have fed a widespread narrative that each country should be solely responsible for its own population only. A global health strategy is strikingly missing as each country races to secure vaccines for its population, even as viruses have no respect for national borders.

The US, for one, has an important leadership role to play. In 2003, the US assumed an important leadership role that led to a successful global drive to combat HIV/AIDS under President George W. Bush's Emergency Plan for AIDS Relief. This time, there have been calls for the US to step up once again and lead in the fight against another global disease, including a suggestion that the Biden administration should use the Defense Production Act to scale up the production of vaccines for other countries, not just the US.

However, the US alone cannot save the world. To complement existing multinational efforts, more could be done multilaterally, particularly by the Group of Seven (G7), an organization of leaders from some of the world's largest economies: Canada, France, Germany, Italy, Japan, the UK, and the US. As a grouping, these powerful economies individually are moving on a path to contain the pandemic, with key vaccine manufacturers located within their borders capable of producing doses beyond what is needed domestically. According to the Center for Strategic and International Studies (2021), the G7 needs to share at least 1 billion (and aim for 2 billion) vaccine doses with low- and middle-income countries by the end of 2021, as well as help more countries distribute and deliver vaccines quickly and equitably across their populations, to achieve at least 60 per cent vaccination coverage in every country in 2022. Beyond developing and committing to a path of vaccine sharing with the rest of the world, other G7 efforts could center on the following:

- establishing a G7 Vaccine Emergency Task Force, open to other nations and organizations, to provide transparency and accountability in the global sharing of vaccines;
- implementing a coordinated G7 strategy to immediately increase the production of vaccines and to boost access by the rest of the world by addressing distribution bottlenecks, removing export barriers, and pooling essential raw materials, equipment, and supplies; and

- accelerating the development of globally distributed manufacturing capacity by connecting public and private sector stakeholders, formalizing voluntary licensing agreements, and establishing cooperative agreements for financing through public and private sources, including the United States International Development Finance Corporation (USDFC), the World Bank's International Finance Corporation (IFC), and local private funding.

Sharing knowledge and removing barriers

Beyond sharing vaccines, there is much mutual benefit to be reaped by sharing ideas, information, best practices, and knowledge. One fundamental approach should address the issue of intellectual property (IP) protections for COVID-19 vaccines in order to pave the way to the removal of import and export restrictions, as well as the loan, release, or donation of vaccine supplies by countries possessing excess supply to low-income countries, whose populations desperately want the vaccines.

This IP protections waiver was first proposed by South Africa and India in October 2021. In 1995, when the World Trade Organization (WTO) was formed, members agreed that in exchange for the lowering of barriers to trade, they would abide by the Agreement on Trade-Related Aspects of Intellectual Property Rights (TRIPS). The WTO can thus invoke a waiver of certain IP rights on technologies that could help combat an exceptional global crisis, such as the COVID-19 pandemic. South Africa and India's proposal sought a WTO waiver for four categories of IP rights—copyright, industrial designs, patents, and undisclosed information—until the majority of the world's population has received effective vaccines and developed immunity to COVID-19. The Biden administration announced in May 2021 that it would support a temporary waiver of IP provisions in the hope that it would allow more developing nations to produce their own COVID-19 vaccines developed by pharmaceutical companies.

The unused capacity in such countries as Bangladesh, Canada, and Israel could easily be turned into vaccine production. Increasing production by sharing technology, knowhow, and other proprietary information should expand the supply of medicines, vaccines, diagnostics, and other technologies, thus helping countries gain access to necessary measures to combat the pandemic. Such a waiver is subject to more negotiations at the WTO. Although more than 100 countries are supportive of the waiver, it has powerful opponents, including the EU and high-income nations, such as Japan and the UK. Opponents suggest that the waiver would discourage future innovation without solving the supply problem because the pharmaceutical industry already has every incentive to produce as much vaccine as it can. Multinational pharmaceutical companies have actively lobbied against the waiver, claiming that companies have yet to make a strong return on their investment—despite data to the contrary.

Establishing bilateral efforts

Bilateral efforts can pave a way toward greater access to COVID-19 vaccines for all. These efforts address existing problems: the lack of global leadership; a weak coordinated global strategy; and COVAX's inability to deliver. On July 6, 2021, Israel and South Korea inked a deal to exchange 700,000 Pfizer-BioNTech COVID-19 vaccine doses. The deal marked the world's first bilateral COVID-19 vaccine swap. Israel will ship 700,000 Pfizer-BioNTech vaccines that are expiring soon to South Korea, and Seoul will return the same number of doses to Israel at a later date. This arrangement could offer a useful template for other countries to manage excess, soon-to-expire vaccines and get them to those in desperate need across the globe sooner.

The pressing vaccine inequity has also opened up opportunities for other forms of bilateral arrangements and, more significantly, the controversial practice of vaccine diplomacy. COVID-19 vaccines have emerged as a new public-diplomacy and nation-branding instrument, as China, India, and Russia, and increasingly the US, compete to project influence through bilateral donations or loans of their home-grown vaccines and the inking of vaccine purchase agreements with countries that have more limited access to vaccines. Leveraging vaccine inequity, China, for one, has targeted low- and middle-income countries left behind as high-income nations scooped up most of the pricier Pfizer-BioNTech and Moderna vaccines, and capitalized on slower-than-hoped-for deliveries by US and European vaccine makers. By March 2021, Beijing had provided millions of free doses to 69 countries and commercially exported many more to 28 other countries. Although China finally joined COVAX in late 2020 after months of hesitation, Beijing is not likely to let up on its vaccine-diplomacy efforts outside of the COVAX framework as long as vaccine inequity exists. China's competitor, India, also donated tens of millions of doses of COVID-19 vaccines to other countries, sparkling criticism that it should have focused on vaccinating its own citizens. In Africa, Russia's Sputnik V vaccine has made significant inroads, competing head-on with China's vaccine-diplomacy efforts. However, China's, India's, and Russia's bilateral vaccine-diplomacy efforts and their outcomes—despite questions over hidden agendas—may help improve vaccine access for more countries. Due to the competition for influence around vaccines among high-income nations, poorer countries could gain earlier access to vaccines.

As the world seeks to overcome the pandemic, many COVID-19 measures to address vaccine inequity, if executed right, are longer-term investments that can pave the way toward more equitable access to global public health. In many poor regions of the world, existing health inequities present structural and systemic challenges that impede COVID-19 control. Pre-COVID-19, 99 per cent of all vaccines used in Africa were imported. Even without COVID-19, it is a moral imperative to build a sustainable framework of global partnerships in technology transfer, infrastructure development, and regulatory management to ensure that no continent or country is left behind when it comes to health—a matter of fundamental import and a basic human right.

References

Center for Strategic and International Studies (2021) Open letter to G7 leaders: a G7 action plan to ensure the world is vaccinated quickly and equitably. June 7. Available at: www.csis.org/analysis/open-letter-g7-leaders-g7-action-plan-ensure-world-vaccinated-quickly-and-equitably

Duke University (no date) Launch and Scale Speedometer: the race for global COVID-19 vaccine inequity. Available at: https://launchandscalefaster.org/COVID-19

United Nations (2021a) Secretary-general calls vaccine equity biggest moral test for global community, as security council considers equitable availability of doses. Available at: https://www.un.org/press/en/2021/sc14438.doc.htm

United Nations (2021b) Unequal vaccine distribution self-defeating, WHO chief tells Economic and Social Council's special ministerial meeting. April 16. Available at: www.un.org/press/en/2021/ecosoc7039.doc.htm

World Health Organization (2021a) Director-general's opening remarks at the media briefing on COVID-19. June 7. Available at: https://www.who.int/director-general/speeches/detail/director-general-s-opening-remarks-at-the-media-briefing-on-covid-19-7-june-2021

World Health Organization (2021b) Vaccine inequity undermining global economic recovery. July 22. Available: https://www.who.int/news/item/22-07-2021-vaccine-inequity-undermining-global-economic-recovery

Further reading

Balfour, H. (2021) Waiving COVID-19 vaccine intellectual property rights. *European Pharmaceutical Review*, June 11. Available at: www.europeanpharmaceuticalreview.com/article/156412/waiving-covid-19-vaccine-intellectual-property-rights/

Burki, T. (2021) Global COVID-19 vaccine inequity. *The Lancet Infectious Diseases*, 21(7): 922–3.

Cohen, J. and Kupferschmidt, K. (2021) Fairer shares: rich countries cornered COVID-19 vaccine doses. *Science*, May 26. Available at: www.sciencemag.org/news/2021/05/rich-countries-cornered-covid-19-vaccine-doses-four-strategies-right-scandalous

Lee, S.T. (2021) Vaccine diplomacy: nation branding and China's COVID-19 soft power play. *Place Branding and Public Diplomacy*. Available at: https://doi.org/10.1057/s41254-021-00224-4

Stulpin, C. (2021) "Shocking imbalance" of COVID-19 vaccine distribution underscores inequity. *Infectious Disease News*, May 20. Available at: www.healio.com/news/infectious-disease/20210514/shocking-imbalance-of-covid19-vaccine-distribution-underscores-inequity

White House (2021) FACT SHEET: Biden–Harris administration is providing at least 80 million COVID-19 vaccines for global use, commits to leading a multilateral effort toward ending the pandemic. May 17. Available at: www.whitehouse.gov/briefing-room/statements-releases/2021/05/17/fact-sheet-biden-harris-administration-is-providing-at-least-80-million-covid-19-vaccines-for-global-use-commits-to-leading-a-multilateral-effort-toward-ending-the-pandemic/

EIGHT

The problem of insecure community health workers in the Global South

Catherine van de Ruit and Amy Zhou

The problem

In many countries in the Global South, there is a profound deficit of medical professionals. For example, World Bank (2017) data for sub-Saharan Africa showed that this region faces one of the worst health worker shortages, with only 0.2 physicians per 1,000 population. In response to these critical shortages, the World Health Organization (WHO) has advocated for the use of community health workers (CHWs) and promoted their occupational development. CHWs are community members whose purpose is to serve as intermediaries between patients in local neighborhoods or villages and the formal health system. They are trained and then tasked with a range of medical and public health services, including peer education and counseling on topics like nutrition, family planning, and disease prevention, as well as basic clinical tasks, such as taking vital signs, filling out patient registries, and monitoring adherence to medications. However, CHWs are seldom recognized as full-time workers deserving of pay, benefits, and occupational safety protections. By replacing trained health professionals with semiskilled CHWs, global health organizations have introduced a temporary solution to address a far more complex problem of health worker scarcity in the Global South.

Both governments and global health organizations recognize the value of CHW programs in expanding access to care. Some countries, such as Brazil and South Africa, have large CHW programs as part of their primary healthcare systems, funded by both national governments and global health organizations. In addition, donors in the global health field heavily fund nongovernmental organizations (NGOs) that rely on CHWs to provide services. CHWs have been especially important in responses to health crises. In response to the HIV epidemic, CHWs provided crucial services like education, counseling, treatment support, and palliative care to patients. Now, during the COVID-19 pandemic, they play a primary role in identifying populations excluded from testing and vaccinations, educating community members about COVID-19 prevention, and assisting with both testing and vaccine rollout.

However, while both governmental and NGO programs rely on CHWs, CHW positions are often precarious. This work is precarious because CHWs occupy an insecure space between formal and informal healthcare. While they provide healthcare services, they are not considered medical professionals because they do not have degrees in medicine or nursing. As community health work is not considered a formal profession, there are few national or international labor regulations in place to standardize or monitor CHW training, salaries, benefits, and working conditions. As a result, many CHWs are underpaid, or even unpaid, and lack access to benefits and workplace protections. This chapter examines challenges with the CHW program model and proposes several paths forward to make community health work more secure and equitable.

Research evidence

While health programs have increasingly relied on CHWs, accurate data on the size of the community health workforce is limited. CHWs are not recognized as healthcare professionals by either governmental agencies or NGOs. As a result, their experiences are often underrepresented in large-scale labor force surveys. In addition, because the work is informal and stops and starts over time, it is difficult for researchers to track the number of CHWs in the labor force. Qualitative research, however, provides important insights into the experiences of CHWs and why this work is often precarious.

Many CHW programs rely on volunteer labor. The global health field has been heavily influenced by what Watkins et al (2012) refer to as the "sustainability doctrine": the idea that international projects are sustainable only if local communities can take them over once donor funds are depleted. From the perspective of donors, creating jobs or paying for local labor is not "sustainable," whereas a volunteer model of community health work could be sustained after donors leave. Governments have also relied on volunteerism. For many low-income countries, structural adjustment policies imposed by the International Monetary Fund and World Bank in the 1980s and 1990s decimated health and welfare systems. In order to meet loan conditions, governments cut spending in healthcare, including worker salaries. Volunteers subsequently helped governments provide care at lower costs because they reduced the need for paid employees.

While CHW programs often offer incentives, such as stipends and training, to encourage volunteers, these incentives do not lead to the long-term professional development or economic security of CHWs. Instead, programs coerce CHWs to participate in healthcare provision for little or no pay. For instance, in Kenneth Maes' (2012) study on CHWs in Ethiopia, the median household per capita income among respondents was US$0.29 per day. CHWs take volunteer positions for many reasons, for instance, they may want to help fellow community members or feel a spiritual calling. However, many CHWs are themselves socioeconomically disadvantaged, so they also hope for paid employment and an escape from poverty. Moreover, CHW programs often take advantage of women's unpaid labor since these roles are associated with expectations that women "naturally" take care of their family members and neighbors. Women living in economically disadvantaged communities may be especially drawn to performing undervalued community health work due to the lack of viable economic alternatives and the hope that these volunteer positions will translate into full-time work. In contexts where populations struggle with poverty, CHW programs become exploitative if very few of these volunteer roles actually convert into secure, paid work. Additionally, CHWs lack formal channels by which they can complain about unfair working conditions or seek recourse to improve work situations. For all of the aforementioned reasons, CHW programs are often beset by low morale, limited efficacy, and high levels of attrition.

Another challenge with CHW programs is their inconsistency. As there are few formal labor regulations for CHWs, salaries, benefits, and the opportunities workers receive can vary tremendously. Many programs rely on a volunteer model, but some offer salaries as well as additional opportunities like training programs, school sponsorship, and travel honorariums. There is limited regulation of international donors and NGOs, so managing organizations are free to establish their own policies. In addition, CHW programs run by NGOs are often short-term because they depend on donor interests and budget cycles. The short-term nature of NGO programs adds to the insecurity that many CHWs in the Global South already face.

Finally, challenges associated with the CHW model are being exacerbated during the COVID-19 pandemic. In addition to the underlying precarity of CHWs' work, reports from several countries, including South Africa, India, and Brazil, show that CHWs receive limited infection–control training and that personal protective equipment supply is inadequate, thus having placed workers' health at grave risk since March 2020.

Recommendations and solutions

International labor and social protection policy

One way to improve the working conditions and livelihoods of CHWs is to leverage international labor and social protection policies. In 2015, the United Nations (UN) added policy guidelines relating to decent job creation, the protection of labor rights, and safe working environments for all workers. These guidelines are now listed as Goal 8 of the UN's Sustainable Development Goals (SDGs) (Decent Work and Economic Growth). The SDGs are a set of international guidelines that the UN uses to hold NGOs and member states accountable for implementing these policies and working toward certain benchmarks. The recent addition of Goal 8 to the SDGs provides an opportunity for NGOs and member states to realign their policies to meet a very specific target: by 2030, countries should realize full and productive employment for all women and men, including young persons and people with disabilities, and provide equal pay for work of equal value.

Taking their lead from the UN, the WHO defined new standards for CHW programs in 2020, urging its member states and international agencies to formally categorize community health work as work. Since the WHO sets policy guidelines and standards for public and private agencies in global health, reforms to policy on CHWs is a significant step in improving the contractual arrangements and labor standards for this occupation. The WHO's new guidelines offer recommendations for CHW selection, training, management, integration, and evaluation. Notably, the WHO strongly recommends remuneration and contracting agreements for CHWs that specify their role, responsibility, working conditions, pay, and rights. The WHO guidelines also suggest developing a career ladder, with opportunities for further education and career development. Although it is too soon to tell how impactful these new WHO guidelines will be, they provide a starting point for governments, international donors, and NGOs to reform their healthcare labor policies.

In addition, other UN agencies can hold global health organizations accountable in their efforts to promote decent and equal work. The Commission on the Status of Women (CSW) is one such UN agency, as it sets international standards promoting gender equality and women's empowerment. In 2021, the CSW devoted its 65th session to encouraging women and girls' full participation in economic and civil life, recognizing that women's household and caregiving responsibilities prevent them from participating in paid work and civic activities. The CSW convention arrived at a set of recommendations to promote gender equality in household responsibilities and prioritize social protection policies—including access to healthcare, education, social services, childcare and maternity, and paternity or parental leave—to encourage women's participation in the labor force. While the CSW agreement focuses on gender equality, these agreements may have positive spillover effects for CHWs. As the WHO pushes for the standardization of CHW programs, recommendations from the CSW agreement bolster WHO efforts by evaluating progress made by NGOs and member states to improve work security and access to safety nets for women currently serving as unpaid or low-paid CHWs.

Integrating CHWs into national healthcare systems

CHWs should also be integrated into the formal workforce within national health systems and NGOs, and, as a result, assigned formal work duties and given job security and benefits like other healthcare professionals. The global turn toward universal health insurance reform has the potential to drive CHW integration. As governments expand access to healthcare, they can include CHWs as part of the formal workforce that provides primary healthcare, especially to marginalized communities. Cases in Brazil and the US provide two models for integrating CHWs into the workforce through health insurance reform.

Following national health insurance reform in 1988, the Brazilian government launched a national CHW program to expand access to care, especially to rural regions. The program organized teams of nurses and CHWs to work in particular geographic areas to provide health education and health promotion, ensure patients' adherence to treatment, and refer patients needing specialist care. While CHWs initially had precarious working conditions, Brazil issued a constitutional amendment in 2006 to recognize CHWs as government employees and formalize the pay scale, work responsibilities, and guidelines for selecting CHWs. Subsequent amendments to the constitution in 2014 and 2018 led to increases in the minimum wage for CHWs and introduced pathways for career promotion.

In the US, the Affordable Care Act (ACA), established in 2010, provided a new funding mechanism that allowed states to integrate CHW programs into the formal workforce. For example, Indiana, Minnesota, and Illinois started their programs by using the ACA's Medicaid expansion. CHW programs connected community members with health and welfare resources, as well as health education, and expanded the availability of outpatient monitoring for various health conditions, including both infectious diseases and long-term chronic conditions. CHW programs also standardized CHW certification and payment so that services can be reimbursed by insurance. Moving forward, further reforms to the ACA are needed to expand and sustain CHW programs. Currently, the ACA payment model privileges clinical procedures, such as working with patients to manage chronic conditions like high blood pressure or diabetes, over addressing structural barriers to care, such as providing transportation and translation services for patients as they visit healthcare facilities. In future reforms, federal and state governments could allow ACA funds to pay for an expanded list of CHW services to conquer a broader range of barriers to care. Additionally, we need stable federal funding streams for CHW programs to ensure that these programs have sustainable futures.

The formal integration of CHWs into the healthcare workforce is also relevant for NGOs on a global scale, that is, standards for CHWs should be uniform across both governmental and nongovernmental sectors. One NGO, Partners in Health, does name CHWs as professionals who are part of the healthcare workforce. Beginning in the early 1980s, Partners in Health has recruited members of local Haitian communities to perform a range of tasks, including: tracing patients experiencing infectious diseases like HIV/AIDS, tuberculosis, and now COVID-19; monitoring patients as they undergo treatment; and accompanying patients for health center visits. They replicated this CHW model in other countries, including Rwanda, Peru, and the US, which helped to accomplish a central mission of the Partners in Health approach: to meet patients where they are by bringing healthcare directly to them. For this program to succeed, Partners in Health followed three principles: (1) CHWs must be recognized as members of the healthcare delivery team, which means they are recruited, paid, and supported for long-term retention; (2) CHWs must be able to connect with and refer patients to other health system professionals; and (3) program budgets must allow for the compensation of community health work by assigning budget line items to CHWs' salary and benefits (for more information on the Partners in Health approach, see Palazuelos et al, 2018). The Partners in Health model demonstrates that offering quality healthcare and achieving social justice are concurrently attainable, and both CHWs and patients can benefit. CHWs were formally recognized for their skill sets and roles in service provision, and they were given adequate pay, benefits, and job security. Data from clinical trials across several countries, analyzing the outcomes of diverse patient conditions like HIV/AIDS treatment, cancer care, and maternal and neonatal care, also indicate how Partner in Health's programs have resulted in positive clinical outcomes for patients. In Haiti, for instance, patients participating in the CHW program had a 100 per cent recovery rate from tuberculosis, in comparison with the government free clinic, which had a 56 per cent recovery rate and a 10 per cent death rate. These data not only show how CHW programs are an important part of the healthcare system, but also suggest that patients receive better care when CHWs' livelihoods are secure.

Social activism and social justice litigation

Finally, grassroots activism builds awareness of the work protections and benefits needed to improve CHWs' quality of life. Workers from some of the world's largest CHW programs have protested their working conditions over time. Many of these movements for workers' rights are ongoing and can provide templates for action for others who are interested in grassroots activism. For instance, India's Accredited Social Health Activists (ASHAs), which has over 1 million CHWs, formed alliances with policy experts from both India and the US. Working together, they pressured the Indian

Health Ministry to improve their working conditions. While they are still working toward achieving occupational status, these efforts led to incremental reforms, such as streamlining the payment system for CHWs, providing more financial support to cover CHWs' transportation costs, and increasing training opportunities. This example shows that leveraging professional networks can help CHW activists achieve some of their goals. Health researchers working on policy issues in any country, especially if focused on workers' rights or healthcare access, can ally themselves with local CHWs to help them negotiate improved working conditions.

Other CHW movements have taken different tactics. In South Africa, CHWs have used social justice litigation and unionization to gain greater recognition. South African CHWs have sought representation from the National Education, Health and Allied Workers' Union and SECTION27, a public interest law center, to petition provincial health ministries to employ CHWs as permanent workers rather than contractors. SECTION27 also supports CHWs by freeing activists arrested during peaceful protests and clearing any criminal records that resulted from the arrests. This is an important legal resource that allows CHWs to fight against efforts from the government to repress protests. These efforts are still ongoing, but they show a promising direction in legal action to secure better working conditions. Additional public interest law centers, whose primary mission is to assist underrepresented groups, could consider representing CHW organizations.

There are also numerous instances of grassroots activism that raise awareness of poor working conditions among CHWs. For instance, in Brazil, CHWs within the *Estratégia Saúde da Família* ('Family Health Strategy' [ESF]) peacefully protested their working conditions on numerous occasions, arguing against the lack of professional development, as well as deficits in training, low pay, and insecure work contracts. Protests have heightened in the face of the COVID-19 pandemic, revealing the limitations of the healthcare system to address this public health crisis, as well as the immense risk that CHWs are facing in the current moment. Outside actors, including the WHO and international donors, have an important role to play in supporting contemporary grassroots activism, as they can place pressure on the Brazilian government to improve working conditions for CHWs in accordance with the Brazilian constitutional amendments and the WHO's SDG guidelines described earlier.

Activist movements in support of increased pay and occupational security for CHWs in Brazil, South Africa, and India highlight how a combination of policy support, legal advocacy, and grassroots mobilization can help CHWs advance their occupational goals. However, these social movements are still emergent. To build on the successes of local worker movements within specific country contexts, CHWs will need to continue to build bridges with other labor organizations, such as unions and political parties aligned to their cause. Additionally, local CHW organizations need help building regional, national, and international networks that can strengthen attempts to ensure that new WHO guidelines are achieved and that CHWs are not only counted as formal members of the workforce, but also granted the full range of benefits that they deserve as healthcare workers in underserved areas.

References

Maes, K. (2012) Volunteerism or labor exploitation? Harnessing the volunteer spirit to sustain AIDS treatment programs in urban Ethiopia. *Human Organization*, 71(1): 54–64.

Palazuelos, D., Farmer, P.E., and Mukherjee, J. (2018) Community health and equity of outcomes: the partners in health experience. *The Lancet Global Health*, 6(5): e491–3.

World Bank (2017) *World Bank Data*. Available at: https://data.worldbank.org/indicator/SH.MED.PHYS.ZS?locations=ZG

Further reading

Chorev, N. (2012) *The World Health Organization between North and South.* Ithaca, NY: Cornell University Press.

Closser, S., Maes, K., Gong, E., Sharma, N., Tesfaye, Y., Abesha, R., Hyman, M., Meyer, N., and Carpenter, J. (2020) Political connections and psychosocial wellbeing among women's development army leaders in rural Amhara, Ethiopia: towards a holistic understanding of community health workers' socioeconomic status. *Social Science & Medicine*, 266: 113373.

Commission on the Status of Women (2021) Women's full and effective participation and decision-making in public life, as well as the elimination of violence, for achieving gender equality and the empowerment of all women and girls. Sixty-fifth session. Available at: https://undocs.org/E/CN.6/2021/L.3

International Labour Organization (2012) *Gender Equality and Decent Work: Selected ILO Conventions and Recommendations Promoting Gender Equality.* Geneva: International Labour Organization.

Lotta, G., Wenham, C., Nunes, J., and Pimenta, D.N. (2020) Community health workers reveal COVID-19 disaster in Brazil. *Lancet*, 396(10248): 365–6.

Mindry, D. (2010) Engendering care: HIV, humanitarian assistance in Africa and the reproduction of gender stereotypes. *Culture, Health & Sexuality*, 12(5): 555–68.

Rai, S.M., Brown, B.D., and Ruwanpura, K.N. (2019) SDG 8: decent work and economic growth—a gendered analysis. *World Development*, 113: 368–80.

Ved, R., Scott, K., Gupta, G., Ummer, O., Singh, S., Srivastava, A., and George, A.S. (2019) How are gender inequalities facing India's one million ASHAs being addressed? Policy origins and adaptations for the world's largest all-female community health worker programme. *Human Resources for Health*, 17(1): 3.

Watkins, S.C., Swidler, A., and Hannan, T. (2012) Outsourcing social transformation: development NGOs as organizations. *Annual Review of Sociology*, 38: 285–315.

WHO (World Health Organization) (2018) WHO guideline on health policy and system support to optimize community health worker programmes. Available at: http://apps.who.int/iris/bitstream/hand le/10665/275474/9789241550369-eng.pdf

WHO (2020) Health workforce policy and management in the context of the COVID-19 pandemic response: interim guidance, 3 December 2020. Available at: https://apps.who.int/iris/handle/10665/337333. License: CC BY-NC-SA 3.0 IGO

NINE

Sub-Saharan Africa's digital poverty in perspective

Ahmed Badawi Mustapha

The problem

The chapter highlights the deficiency in Sub-Saharan Africa's (SSA's) Internet access. The Internet has become an integral part of almost all human endeavors. People use it in multifaceted ways to such an extent that practically all aspects of human life connect in some way to the Internet. Recognizing this fact, in 2016, the United Nations (UN) passed a nonbinding resolution to declare the disruption of Internet access a violation of human rights. Even though disruption is deliberate in many instances, in SSA, the problem remains that much of the population has inadequate access.

The UN's Sustainable Development Goals (SDGs) acknowledge how "the spread of information and communication technology and global interconnectedness has great potential to accelerate human progress and to develop knowledge societies" (ITU Council, 2020). Currently, access to the Internet, or the lack of it, directly impacts productivity and social well-being. Access is not an issue for most advanced countries, as the Internet is accessible and affordable, if not free. Numerous reports attest to the fact that equitable access to the Internet could massively transform most parts of Africa (see Bahia et al, 2020, 2021; Masaki et al, 2020).

However, the narrative is different in many parts of the world, especially in SSA. Inadequate Internet access is a preexisting problem, but COVID-19 exposed how unprepared the SSA region has been for increased reliance on the Internet to keep affairs running. This chapter regards this inadequacy of Internet connectivity as a form of "digital poverty." The exceptional nature of this poverty, compared to the usual economic poverty, is that in SSA, one may be financially capable but unable to access the Internet due to poor infrastructure, no matter how ready a person may be to pay for it.

The chapter first reviews some evidence supporting the deficient nature of the Internet in SSA. What follows is a discussion on how to mitigate the problem through recommendations and strategies for governments and other stakeholders in the SSA information and communication technology (ICT) industry. The chapter takes the view that resolving the Internet deficit on the continent would require a multidimensional approach. However, a strategic starting point toward alleviating SSA's digital poverty would be vastly improving Internet (especially broadband) infrastructure, while enhancing the affordability of services and electronic gadgets.

Research evidence

SSA's struggle for reliable and affordable Internet access is not new. However, the advent of COVID-19 and the necessary lockdown measures led to complete reliance on the Internet for almost everything, including work and education, thereby exposing digital inequalities in SSA. A November 2020 World Bank Report, *Measuring Internet Access in Sub-Saharan Africa* (Frankfurter et al, 2020), presented three key findings:

- "household Internet access may be less prevalent than commonly believed";
- "access rates are particularly low for rural and poorer households"; and
- "many people in SSA access the Internet through mobile phones rather than a home computer."

According to a study by the Pew Research Center conducted in 2018, the global median of Internet usage is 75 per cent; however, while an advanced country like South Korea scored 96 per cent, which is in the upper percentile, African countries scored below 40 per cent, with Tanzania at the bottom, scoring 25 per cent (Pew Research Center, 2018). As research conducted by the World Bank has indicated, most people in SSA access the Internet through mobile phones. However, overall mobile connectivity is also deficient in the region. According to the Global System for Mobile Communication's 2021 mobile connectivity report, despite the data showing more than half of the world using mobile internet, SSA remains the region with the largest usage gap in connectivity (those living in areas where there is no broadband coverage available), with a rate of 19 per cent.[1] The report also highlighted issues and challenges related to digital literacy, infrastructure, affordability, consumer readiness, and content and services. With all of these put together, it was no surprise that the COVID-19 lockdowns hindered education and business activities in SSA to a larger extent than other regions in the world.

The poor nature of Internet access in various sectors, particularly in education and among younger individuals, is well documented by a study jointly conducted by the United Nations Children's Fund and the International Communication Union (UNICEF and ITU, 2020), which indicated that most households and schools lack Internet connectivity. For instance, in West and Central Africa, only 5 per cent of younger people below age 25 have access to the Internet at home, while 3 per cent of the same age group in Southern and Eastern Africa have Internet access at home (UNICEF and ITU, 2020). In relative terms, 59 per cent of younger people of the same age in Eastern Europe and Central Asia have access to the Internet in their homes (UNICEF and ITU, 2020). These figures reflect the situation of Internet access in homes in the region when most educational institutions across the globe have switched to online teaching and learning. A total of 65 per cent of children and young people (2.2 billion youth and children aged 25 or less) were without Internet access at home globally (UNICEF and ITU, 2020). However, the disparity and the deficiency are starker in SSA. Faced with this reality, it is no surprise that millions of young people and students in SSA find it difficult to cope with the global trend of switching online. In some countries like Ghana, teenage pregnancies and other social vices soared as the school-going youth remained unsupported.[2]

Independently, for over a decade, the ITU has been reporting the Internet deficit observed in the least developed countries (LDCs), most of which are in SSA. Recognizing the need to act, it sponsored a series of conferences and summits, partnering with key stakeholders like the African Union, the UN, and the World Bank. Data collated and shared by the ITU highlighted that Africa has the lowest Internet access per household. Compared to 82 per cent of households having the Internet as of 2015 in Europe, only about 10.7 per cent of households had the Internet in SSA, highlighting the profound nature of SSA's digital poverty.[3]

Recommendations and solutions

There is a need for comprehensive policy options and actions regarding how to mitigate the problem and, ultimately, significantly improve the situation. There are several areas to tackle, such as infrastructure development, the affordability of equipment and mobile devices (such as smartphones or computers), and Internet services. In this regard, existing global initiatives like the Broadband Commission for Sustainable Development, spearheaded by the United Nations Educational, Scientific, and Cultural Organization (UNESCO) and the ITU, need to be commended and supported by various stakeholders (ITU and UNESCO, 2020). The commission's initiatives and recommendations are comprehensive and could be integrated in SSA countries' national policies toward improving broadband connectivity and public Internet access. The commission sets the tone for a broader discussion on how to mitigate the problem, considering the global nature of the membership of the organizations involved in the initiative. Both UNESCO and the ITU have over 190 member countries, which makes their initiative far-reaching. Any recommendation and solution to the issues relating to digital poverty in various parts of the world, especially SSA, must build on an existing initiative that is widely inclusive and has a massive following. The three significant pillars proposed by the Broadband Commission for Sustainable Development's agenda for action over the next decade are highlighted in the following passages, together with how they could be extended to fit in with local regional dynamics. These pillars are resilient connectivity, affordable access, and safe use (ITU and UNESCO, 2020).

Resilient connectivity

This pillar aims to ensure uninterrupted connectivity and access to the Internet through a robust broadband infrastructure. The action plan recognizes the need for a robust infrastructure to help achieve this, in terms of increasing bandwidth and supporting all populations to be connected. In line with this target, a practical way to ensure that it is realized in the context of SSA (and perhaps beyond) is for subregional governments to be in control of ownership and infrastructure; and grant tax exemptions on infrastructural equipment.

Be in control of ownership and infrastructure

For resilient, robust, and broader connectivity to be meaningful, local governments need to be able to regulate ownership and set up the required infrastructure for an incessant performance. However, for the most part, because the telecommunication companies operating in the SSA region are fully privatized or partly owned by the states, governments in the region are rendered powerless over the essentials in terms of operation. In 2009, Vodafone acquired 70 per cent of Ghana Telecom, with Ghana maintaining only a 30 per cent stake. Likewise, Orange acquired 51 per cent of Telekom Kenya in 2007.[4] The main reason for privatization is mostly nonperformance due to most SSA governments' inability to manage these national entities well. Many African countries have, in one way or another, opened their telecommunication entities for private investment. While this could be a positive step in ensuring quality service provision and the expansion of cellular networks, most governments lose operational leverage over telecommunication entities in their countries. Privatization of crucial entities like state-owned telecommunication enterprises need to be time-bound (for example, for five to ten years), after which there could be a reevaluation of the ownership structure. Situating this within the Broadband Commission for Sustainable Development's initiative, such a reevaluation by regional governments needs to not only ensure resilient connectivity, but also aim at granting most of its citizenry access to the internet.

Grant tax exemptions on infrastructural equipment

Investing in infrastructure is key to achieving resilient connectivity and extending it to cover the rural population. Private telecommunication companies (in whole or partial ownership) invest solely for profitability, not to serve the citizenry. They primarily invest in densely populated areas due to the higher penetration rate leading to higher profitability. This adversely affects the Internet connectivity of rural people and the less privileged in most SSA countries because infrastructural investments do not target them. Rather than focusing so much on tax revenues from these telecommunication companies, governments in the region could reduce the tax rate on erecting masts and laying cables to rural areas in order to encourage telecommunication companies to invest in those areas toward expanding connectivity. Telecommunication companies making entry into SSA markets could receive temporary tax relief for the gadgets and equipment they import to strengthen and widen Internet connectivity at homes. The time-bound nature of it would prevent abuse by those firms investing in the telecommunication sector. Additionally, to make electronics, especially personal computers (desktops or laptops) affordable, their import taxes must be reviewed while strongly regulating the prices within respective countries in the region. SSA governments could categorize any infrastructural equipment essential items, thereby lessening the importation cost of such equipment.

Affordable access

Affordability of services and devices feature prominently in the action plan of the Broadband Commission for Sustainable Development. Service discounts and price reductions for devices are vital toward achieving this action plan. Most importantly, affordability must be tied to corporate social responsibility.

Affordability and corporate social responsibility

SSA governments need to hold telecommunication companies accountable and push them toward making Internet accessibility affordable as an integral part of their social responsibilities in the countries they operate in. However, relying solely on governments might not be sufficient. Intergovernmental organizations and developmental partners should be engaged. They could prioritize and have concrete action on Internet connectivity as an integral part of loans, grants, or aid to SSA countries. Such practices would urge governments across the region to make digitization policies a key area of priority. There is the need for advocacy that would extend the social responsibility of telecommunication companies to massively include granting educational institutions heavily subsidized, if not free, broadband, Internet connectivity, and gadgets. There have been some strides in this regard, but COVID-19 exposed the existing deficit and the need to do more. In terms of affordability, most telecommunication companies currently operating in Africa set up their masts on individual properties in residential areas and grant the property owners some monetary compensation. In addition to such compensation, governments could ensure the inclusion of a radius that is set up when erecting a mast to allow several households within this radius to access the Internet freely or at a highly subsidized rate.

Tax regulation of mobile devices to favor the less privileged

The affordability of services and electronics like phones and laptops is strongly connected with taxation. SSA governments could help regulate service prices by significantly reducing the cost of entry into the telecommunication sector to attract new entrants. To help fill the gap in Internet connectivity, import duties and taxation on mobile gadgets and broadband routers need to be very low or receive heavy subsidies. This measure would help reduce the price of devices for Internet access.

Safe use for informed and educated societies

The action plan focuses on the safety of Internet users, especially children and the vulnerable. It aims to protect users' privacy and ensure they have adequate and accurate information on online content of interest. Indeed, after working on resilient connectivity and affordable access, there is the need to build confidence in using various online platforms in the citizenry. Telecommunication companies, in partnerships with governments, need to pay particular attention to the presubscription and aftersales customer services of various Internet providers. New subscribers could be inducted into some safety tips while online. This needs to be augmented with the usage of various media avenues available to continue educating users on issues relating to online safety. Regional governments need to regulate the protection of consumers' or citizens' data through appropriate policies that prioritize their safety online.

Conclusion

Confronting digital poverty, especially in less developed regions like SSA, could help transform the region in many ways. It could help alleviate the abject poverty and the low level of literacy bedeviling the region. Adequate policies adopted in tackling the problem must be far-reaching and inclusive. Toward this end, there is a need for concerted efforts by governmental institutions, regional institutions, and international organizations. In this regard, the Broadband Commission for Sustainable Development's initiative to help curb the situation in the coming decade sets the context, and it is worth considering and adapting to suit regional contexts and dynamics toward ultimately salvaging many parts of the world from "digital poverty."

Notes

1. See: https://www.gsma.com/r/wp-content/uploads/2021/09/The-State-of-Mobile-Internet-Connectivity-Report-2021.pdf
2. See: www.wvi.org/stories/ghana/sexual-exploitation-during-lockdown-ghana
3. See: www.itu.int/en/ITU-D/Statistics/Dashboards/Pages/IFF.aspx
4. See: https://pastel.archives-ouvertes.fr/tel-01502810/document

References

Bahia, K., Castells, P., Cruz, G., Masaki, T., Pedros, X., Pfutze, T., Rodriguez-Castelan, C., and Winkler, H. (2020) *The Welfare Effects of Mobile Broadband Internet: Evidence from Nigeria*. Policy Research Working Paper No. 9230. Washington, DC: World Bank. Available at: https://openknowledge.worldbank.org/handle/10986/33712

Bahia, K., Castells, P., Cruz, G., Masaki, T., Rodriguez-Castelan, C., and Sanfelice, V. (2021) *Mobile Broadband Internet, Poverty and Labor Outcomes in Tanzania*. Policy Research Working Paper No. 9749. Washington, DC: World Bank. Available at: https://openknowledge.worldbank.org/handle/10986/36172

Frankfurter, Z., Kokoszka, K., Newhouse, D., Silwal, A.R., and Tian, S. (2020) *Measuring Internet Access in Sub-Saharan Africa*. Poverty and Equity Notes No. 31. Washington, DC: World Bank. Available at: https://openknowledge.worldbank.org/handle/10986/34302

ITU (International Telecommunication Union) and UNESCO (United Nations Educational, Scientific, and Cultural Organization) (2020) *The State of Broadband 2020: Tackling Digital Inequalities: A Decade for Action*. Geneva: ITU and UNESCO. Available at: www.itu.int/dms_pub/itu-s/opb/pol/S-POL-BROADBAND.21-2020-PDF-E.pdf

ITU Council (2020) International Telecommunication Union Administrative Council (ITU Council): general introduction. Available at: https://sustainabledevelopment.un.org/index.php?page=view&type=30022&nr=1932&menu=3170

Masaki, T., Granguillhome Ochoa, R., and Rodriguez-Castelan, C. (2020) *Broadband Internet and Household Welfare in Senegal*. Policy Research Working Paper No. 9386. Washington, DC: World Bank. Available at: https://openknowledge.worldbank.org/handle/10986/34472

Pew Research Center (2018) Internet connectivity seen as having positive impact on life in sub-Saharan Africa. October. Available at: www. pewresearch.org/global/2018/10/09/internet-connectivity-seen-as-having-positive-impact-on-life-in-sub-saharan-africa/

UNICEF (United Nations Children's Fund) and (International Telecommunication Union) (2020) *How Many Children and Young People Have Internet Access at Home? Estimating Digital Connectivity During the COVID-19 Pandemic.* New York, NY: UNICEF. Available at: https://data.unicef.org/resources/children-and-young-people-internet-access-at-home-during-covid19/

Further reading

Aikins, S.K. (2019) Determinants of digital divide in Africa and policy implications. *International Journal of Public Administration in the Digital Age (IJPADA)*, 6(1): 64–79.

Arakpogun, E.O., Elsahn, Z., Nyuur, R.B., and Olan, F. (2020) Threading the needle of the digital divide in Africa: the barriers and mitigations of infrastructure sharing. *Technological Forecasting & Social Change*, 161: 121637. https://doi.org/10.1016/j.techfore.2020.120263

Figueiredo, M., Prado, P., and Kramer, M. (2012) Overcoming poverty through digital inclusion. *IT Professional*, 14(3): 6–10.

Gebremichael, M.D. and Jackson, J.W. (2006) Bridging the gap in sub-Saharan Africa: a holistic look at information poverty and the region's digital divide. *Government Information Quarterly*, 23(2): 267–80.

Ragnedda, M. (2017) *The Third Digital Divide: A Weberian Approach to Digital Inequalities.* Abingdon: Routledge.

Ragnedda, M. and Muschert, G.W. (eds) (2013) *The Digital Divide: The Internet and Social Inequality in International Perspective.* Abingdon: Routledge.

Ragnedda, M. and Muschert, G.W. (eds) (2017) *Theorizing Digital Divides.* Abingdon: Routledge.

Thompson, K.M., Jaeger, P.T., Greene Taylor, N., Subramaniam, M., and Bertot, J.C. (2014) *Digital Literacy and Digital Inclusion: Information Policy and the Public Library.* Lanham, MD: Rowman & Littlefield.

UNICEF (n.d.). Project Connect: Mapping School Connectivity Globally. Retrieved March 30, 2022, from https://projectconnect.unicef.org/map

TEN

Climate change, migration, and language endangerment in the Pacific

Jason Brown and John Middleton

The problem

Climate change is disproportionately affecting Pacific nations, in part, due to their fragile island environments. This change indirectly threatens Pacific *languages*, with a mass migration of populations occurring and climate-related language policy still in its infant stage. This work aims to outline the problems and prospects for policy development in this area, with an aim to solving the associated problem of language loss through migration.

The consequences of climate change are vast for small islands and atolls. However, a common misconception is that migration out of a region for climate change only occurs when low-lying areas become uninhabitable due to rising sea levels. This phenomenon is indeed a significant danger; for example, it is conceivable that atolls like Tokelau and Tuvalu, whose highest points are, respectively, only 5 m and 4.6 m above sea level, are in immediate danger of being overcome by the sea. Due to the large circumference of the atolls and their overall low elevation, even a fraction of sea-level rise will disproportionately decrease the land available for habitation. However, while a genuine threat, the "sinking" of these atolls is perhaps a lesser overall concern. There are much broader effects of climate change that influence and motivate the migration of indigenous people away from their homelands. Higher average global temperatures cause increases in climate variability, meaning rainfall patterns, temperature, and cyclones become more variable and less predictable. With a significant weather event, the fresh water on a small island or atoll can be contaminated, destroying its natural water source for days. The apparent consequence is that although these locales are still technically inhabitable, growing crops and maintaining a consistent freshwater supply becomes increasingly difficult.

To escape from these hardships, including the related threats to financial health, many people choose to migrate. In the short term, migration may be restricted to individuals and families, but whole communities may need to migrate as time passes. Migration caused by climate change is estimated to reach 200 million by 2050 (Campbell and Warrick, 2014).

Climate change intersects with the problem of language death. Migration itself is not necessarily a factor in language loss. Typically, when members of a language population leave the community, a population that speaks the language remains in the homeland, meaning the language is maintained. That is not to say that the use of these migrant languages will not reduce because of outside pressures, such as political, social, or economic factors (Romaine, 1989; Schmidt, 1990; Pawley, 1991). However, with the potential loss of the homeland, languages will be forced to migrate to another part of the world. When a language is nondominant in a community, pressures on the language become exacerbated, such as negative perceptions of the language and inequalities between speakers, leading to the decline of the vernacular and threatening its vitality (Tsunoda, 2006). In the Pacific, the increase in environmental refugees is an emerging issue, which directly affects the endangerment of languages in this part of the world.

There are a significant number of threats to the existence of languages. With around 6,000 languages overall, the vast majority (95 per cent) of the world's languages are spoken by only 5 per cent of the population (Crystal, 2000). This dynamic means a tiny population of people speak most languages, so any destruction in their habitat, livelihoods, or culture could send a language toward endangerment and possibly extinction. Estimates are that 20–50 per cent of the world's 6,000 languages are moribund, 40–75 per cent are weakening, and only 5–10 per cent are safe (Krauss, 1992, 1998). Language death presents a critical problem related to the loss of human diversity and loss of identity. The loss of a language is paralleled by the loss of a species and loss of biodiversity. Language death amounts to the irretrievable loss of indigenous knowledge (including ethnobiological knowledge), ways of understanding the world, and people's lifeways. Not only is this a problem for science, but it is a social problem, as the loss of one's language also constitutes the erosion of one's identity.

Language death has dramatically increased during the era of globalization. The expected rate of language death averages out at one language dying every two weeks (Crystal, 2000). Despite this, language death is surprisingly rare in the Pacific given the diversity of languages in this region. For instance, of the languages spoken in the Solomon Islands, Taiwan, Papua New Guinea, Micronesia, and Polynesia (which is a representative sampling), only 305 are threatened, with 59 seriously endangered (Wurm, 2003). It is, however, well known that island environments are incredibly fragile. Climate change in the Pacific translates into climate variability, where rainfall patterns, temperature, and cyclones become more variable and less predictable (Campbell and Warrick, 2014). Consequently, the Pacific faces a new threat, unique in terms of the world's languages: environmental destruction of atolls and islands, causing the migration of people and the subsequent loss of language and culture.

Research evidence

To better understand the dynamics involved in climate-based migration in the Pacific and how this impacts the vitality of languages, two case studies are outlined here. First, Halia is an Austronesian language spoken in the Carteret Islands, comprised of six small islands 86 km away from the mainland of Bougainville Island. The islands are politically part of the Autonomous Region of Bougainville, Papua New Guinea. Estimates are that there are 2,500 Halia speakers in the Carterets. Due to the tiny land area of the atolls (0.6 km^2) and low elevation (1.2 m above sea level at the highest point), sea-level rise is a significant issue (Edwards, 2013). Talks of relocations and several attempts for mass migration have occurred since the 1970s. In 2006, a relocation strategy was formed for 1,700 Carteret Islanders to relocate to the mainland of Bougainville to live on land donated by the Roman Catholic Church (Peisa, 2011).

Issues with the planned migration were widespread. Among these was the issue of landownership, which does not resemble Western ideals of land that can be bought and sold (Petit, 2011). Further problems came from trauma the islanders experienced by leaving behind their land and culture. Despite these factors affecting the actual migration, one critical point in this case study is that Halia is also spoken (by an estimated 17,500 people) on the mainland in the area chosen for relocation. This dynamic makes the situation unique, in that the climate-caused migration allowed the Carteret Islanders to move to a land where their language is native. While the islands are in danger of becoming uninhabitable, the language itself is less under threat due to its existence on the mainland. When climate change causes people to relocate, the danger is when there is no physical landmass where the language natively occurs. In the case of Halia, there are many obstacles for relocation to occur. However, one less problematic factor is that the targeted relocation area has Halia as the native language. This relocation example highlights a case where climate-influenced migration may be more successful in language maintenance.

In contrast, with around 4,000 speakers, Tokelauan is an endangered language, only spoken (by about 1,500) as the dominant language in the Tokelau Islands. The physical landmass of Tokelau comprises three atolls, Atafu, Nukunonu, and Fakaofo, with a combined total of 12 km^2. Of important note is that the entire nation is less than 5 m above sea level (Lefale, Faiva, Anderson, 2017). The risk of climate change for Tokelau has been deemed critical since the 1990s (McLean and d'Aubert, 1993). Sea levels have risen, and there has been an increased frequency and intensity of extreme weather events like cyclones, which threaten the existence of the atolls themselves. Like all examples of climate problems in island communities, rising seawater is just one issue. Scarce freshwater sources, diminished crop survival, and the lack of drinkable water are further threats to the islanders' livelihoods. A major weather event, such as a cyclone, is a severe short-term threat, just as the rising sea levels are a serious long-term one. As such, migration is a genuine option for Tokelauans living in the islands.

Today, more Tokelauan speakers (totaling around 2,500) live in New Zealand than the atolls themselves. This fact is partly due to the close relationship between the countries: Tokelauan is a non-self-governing territory of New Zealand, meaning that access to New Zealand for Tokelauans is relatively easy. The migration of this language across to the more stable landmass of New Zealand is a trend that will only continue with the decreasing inhabitability of the atolls. In New Zealand, there is little policy for the protection and maintenance of the language, with the front line of language maintenance sitting mainly with the communities themselves.

Simply put, the environmental factors that threaten the existence of the atolls pressure the languages spoken there too. The examples discussed here illustrate the potential for a migration and language crisis. While the languages are still being maintained in these cases, it is easy to understand how as the climate situation becomes more extreme, language loss is inevitable due to climate migration.

Recommendations and solutions

These two cases share certain core similarities but differ concerning the language makeup of the new homeland and the level of policy in place to protect these migrants. These cases have been selected not only because they are typical in regards to the larger problem, but also because atoll nations are on the front lines of the climate crisis. While the effects of climate change are global, few experience these effects as directly as those living in low-lying atolls and island nations. This is not an experience limited to the Pacific, as indigenous and nonindigenous populations in other regions also grapple with climate change. What is seen in the Pacific can easily be connected to places like the Mississippi River delta region in Louisiana (for example, Isle de Jean Charles, elevation 61 cm, where the Biloxi-Chitimacha-Choctaw are being resettled) or the Maldives in the Indian Ocean. Thus, resettlement projects will be a necessary long-term solution in many areas of the world.

The intricacies of this situation require several policies to address the problem. An obvious solution is a preventive climate change policy that attempts to reverse or slow down the effects of climate change. Much has been written about this type of policy development across various regions globally, and we will not focus further on this topic here.

Policy measures must address the migration of people due to climate change. Within the policy, climate refugees' movement and the protection of their languages must be ensured (as guaranteed by the Declaration of Human Rights), and these policies are currently lacking (Glahn, 2009). Some countries, such as New Zealand, are better placed to provide a haven for climate refugees in the Pacific than others. Tokelau is a New Zealand protectorate, and all Tokelauans automatically receive New Zealand citizenship, meaning that migration policy to and from the atolls is already sanctioned. However, with increasing political instability in the Pacific islands, the difficulty in creating policy to protect indigenous languages also increases. In Tokelau's case, a proposal for independence from New Zealand has been discussed for years, which, if passed, would create complications for climate refugees from the atolls. Furthermore, under current policy, recognition and maintenance of the Tokelauan language needs strengthening through New Zealand government policy as migration increases.

Even the infrastructure to support climate refugees in other Pacific nations is problematic, as illustrated by the Carteret Islands. The relocation site for the Carteret Islanders is in the Autonomous Region of Bougainville, which is in the middle of significant government upheaval, having voted in a referendum to become independent from Papua New Guinea. There is ineffective socioeconomic planning for the relocated islanders. Under the current legal framework, Bougainville remains an autonomous region, potentially reducing the power for Bougainville to provide land for the refugees (Displacement Solutions, 2008).

Language revitalization is another process that requires specific policies from governments to address. Language revitalization has mainly addressed protecting and promoting indigenous languages; never before has there been such a reason to promote the revitalization of displaced languages that are not native to that nation-state. Critically, for a country like New Zealand, where there is comprehensive policy covering the indigenous Māori language, the policy is not fully enacted to protect languages not indigenous to New Zealand. The needed policy must include languages that are not native to the country, which puts policymakers in a sensitive position. On the one hand, the country's policy must vigorously address the indigenous language due to its endangered status. However, on the other hand, there must also be an attempt to protect languages that have arrived through climate change migration. There is little anticipating how many or which languages will end up settling in the country as migrants in many contexts.

A commonly agreed-upon diagnostic for assessing language endangerment is the United Nations Educational, Scientific, and Cultural Organization's methodology for assessing *language vitality* and endangerment, created in the early 2000s (Ad Hoc Expert Group on Endangered Languages, 2003). These diagnostics include: (1) the absolute number of speakers; (2) the proportion of speakers within the total population; (3) intergenerational language transmission; (4) community members' attitudes toward their language; (5) shifts in the domains of language use; (6) governmental and institutional language attitudes and policies, including official status and language use; (7) the type and quality of documentation; (8) responses to new domains and media; and (9) the availability of materials for language education and literacy. These nine factors can also apply to policies on language revitalization, such that increasing each factor will protect the vitality of any given language. This therefore provides a framework for policy to be developed and implemented. A policy that considers all aspects of a language has more chance of protecting the language's health in the long term, even if it resides in a country where it did not originate.

Many of the policies created for indigenous languages are unlikely to be applied to "displaced" languages. Such policy as using the language in government and mass media, or even in business, is unlikely to gain traction. As such, native citizens may not have the same patriotism or positive attitudes toward these displaced languages. However, a policy can promote language use within the displaced community, allowing the language to become embedded into the national psyche. For example, Reyhner et al's (1999: vi–vii) recommendations for languages that are used within a community are as follows: "Offer literacy in minority language. Promote voluntary programs in the school and other community institutions to improve the prestige and use of the language. Use language in local government functions, especially social services. Give recognition to special local efforts through awards, etc." These recommendations could work equally well for native indigenous languages as displaced languages.

The balancing act between indigenous language policy and displaced language policy is critical. New Zealand policy with regard to the indigenous Māori language is advanced. A language strategy has been laid out, which includes recognizing Māori as an official language and providing financial support for promotion of the language. A key focus has been on "language nests," which involve Māori language preschools, meaning nonfluent parents are able to provide their children with the opportunity to learn the language. This policy has been successful, not only in New Zealand, but also in Hawaii for the Hawaiian language. While the focus has remained on ethnically Māori people to revitalize their language, more recently, it has become recognized that non-Māori may be more included in this policy than before. In fact, the language has become part of the New Zealand identity for all New Zealanders, hence the increased positive attitudes toward the language by non-Māori.

This demonstrates what type of policy might be adopted for displaced languages to thrive. While it may be straightforward to place the burden of language maintenance on its people, bringing the language to *all* people in the host country will be vital. Financing language preschools is a strong way to support the displaced language. Not only does this provide a place for the youth of the displaced people to learn the language, but it also allows the language to be learned by the children of the host nation. Increasing the accessibility of language learning will provide a platform for host-nation citizens to hear the language, increasing positive attitudes toward the displaced group. As time passes, such policies as official recognition of the language and use in mass media become possible due to the change in attitudes of the host nation. If the peoples of the host country look at the displaced language as one of their own, treating the language as semi-indigenous becomes significantly easier.

Finally, legal action is a possible solution. Torres Strait Islanders are currently taking legal action against the Australian government, claiming that the protection of communities against climate change is a legal obligation (where the basis of the claim is identity and culture). The Australian federal government oversees the Torres Strait Islands, meaning that this legal pathway is accessible. This claim is being modelled on a similar claim from a group in the Netherlands who took legal action, and won, against the government there. This action was to protect the citizens of the country from climate change, and the subsequent action from the Dutch government reduced carbon emissions significantly. For islands like those in the Torres Strait, such actions as reducing carbon emissions may be too late in terms of protecting the languages there. However, the precedent has been set for legal action against a government on climate change. As such, we suggest that legal action is a possible pathway for displaced communities to obtain funding for the protection of their islands and their languages. If the endangered nation is under the protectorate of a larger government, as Tokelau, the Cook Islands, and Niue are for New Zealand, legal action may force the hand of the larger state to support these languages in its territory. This could be through the creation of language schools, the promotion of the language in the media, and the use of the language in formal settings. The case studies outlined earlier illustrate that climate-induced migration and the resulting threat to Pacific languages require immediate attention, particularly concerning policy relating to both migration and language maintenance.

References

Ad Hoc Expert Group on Endangered Languages (2003) Language vitality and endangerment. Document adopted by the International Expert Meeting on UNESCO Programme Safeguarding of Endangered Languages Paris, March 10–12.

Campbell, J. and Warrick, O. (2014) Climate change and migration issues in the Pacific. PhD dissertation, United Nation Economic and Social Commission for Asia and the Pacific Office.

Crystal, D. (2000) *Language Death*. Cambridge: Cambridge University Press.

Displacement Solutions (2008) The Bougainville Resettlement Initiative meeting report. Canberra, Australia, December 11.

Edwards, J.B. (2013) The logistics of climate-induced resettlement: lessons from the Carteret Islands, Papua New Guinea. *Refugee Survey Quarterly*, 32(3): 52–78.

Glahn, B. (2009) *Climate Refugees? Addressing the International Legal Gaps*. London: The International Bar Association, June 11.

Krauss, M. (1992) The world's languages in crisis. *Language*, 68(1): 4–10.

Krauss, M. (1998) The scope of the language endangerment crisis and recent response to it. *Studies in Endangered Languages. ICHEL Linguistic Studies* 1: 101–13.

Lefale, P.F., Faiva, P., and Anderson, C.L. (2017) *Living with Change (LivC): An Integrated National Strategy for Enhancing the Resilience of Tokelau to Climate Change and Related Hazards, 2017–2030*. Wellington, New Zealand: Government of Tokelau and LeA International Consultants, Ltd.

McLean, R. and d'Aubert, A.M. (1993) Implications of climate change and sea level rise for Tokelau. South Pacific Regional Environment Programme, SPREP Reports and Studies Series 61.

Pawley, A. (1991) Vanishing languages of the Pacific: what price progress? Revised text of seminar presentation, Australian National University, April 3.

Peisa, T. (2011) Carterets integrated relocation program, Bougainville, Papua New Guinea, project proposal. Available at: www.newday.com/sites/default/files/resources/4.%20Carterets%20Relocation%20Program.pdf

Petit, M. (2011) Reducing emissions from deforestation and degradation: human rights and the commodification of carbon. *Asia Pacific Journal of Environmental Law*, 14: 87–104.

Reyhner, J., Cantoni, G., St. Clair, R., and Yazzie, E.P. (eds) (1999) *Revitalizing Indigenous Languages*. Flagstaff, AZ: Northern Arizona University.

Romaine, S. (1989) Pidgins, creoles, immigrant, and dying languages. In N.C. Dorian (ed) *Investigating Obsolescence: Studies in Language Contraction and Death*. Cambridge: Cambridge University Press, pp 369–83.

Schmidt, A. (1990) *The Loss of Australia's Aboriginal Language Heritage*. Canberra: Aboriginal Studies Press.

Tsunoda, T. (2006) *Language Endangerment and Language Revitalization: An Introduction*. Berlin: De Gruyter Mouton.

Wurm, S.A. (2003) The language situation and language endangerment in the Greater Pacific area. *Amsterdam Studies in the Theory and History of Linguistic Science Series*, 4: 15–48.

ELEVEN

Reimagining the climate crisis as a social crisis

Marko Salvaggio

The problem

On 14 March, 2019, Cyclone Idai—one of the worst tropical cyclones ever to hit southern Africa—made landfall near the port city of Beira in central Mozambique, before moving across the southeast African region, affecting millions of people in Mozambique, Malawi, and Zimbabwe. Six weeks later, Cyclone Kenneth made landfall in northern Mozambique, making it the first time in recorded history that two strong tropical cyclones hit the country in the same season. The devastation caused by Idai and Kenneth left more than 1,300 people dead, with many more missing, and 2.5 million people in need of basic resources and humanitarian assistance (for healthcare, nutrition, protection, education, water, and sanitation) in Mozambique alone (UNICEF, 2019). Today, over 104,000 people continue to live in resettlement sites and accommodation centers in central Mozambique, and nearly 670,000 people are displaced in the northern part of the country (CARE, 2021). But were these two "natural disasters," which are deemed part of the "climate crisis," the root cause of this tragedy?

Since 2010, the French energy firm Total has invested US\$20 billion in a liquefied natural gas project just off the coast of northern Mozambique, making it one of the biggest investments in Africa. Supported by the World Bank and International Monetary Fund (IMF), as well as the Mozambican government, this gas project is estimated to produce 65 trillion cubic feet of recoverable natural gas by 2024 and will expand to produce 43 million tonnes per annum. The gas will be liquefied and exported to wealthy nations, including the US and Canada, where it will then be used as a fuel for the energy and transportation sectors, as well as a raw material to produce chemicals and fertilizers for the agricultural sector. Revenue gained through this project raises the hope that Mozambique—one of the economically poorest countries in the world—will catapult to middle-income status by the mid-2030s and be able to develop a national infrastructure that could help to withstand future disasters (Elston and Darby, 2020).

Yet, while many Mozambicans suffer from the effects of annual tropical storms, the process by which natural gas is extracted and transported off the coast of their country leaks methane into the atmosphere. A growing body of climate science research suggests that methane—a greenhouse gas that accounts for about 20 per cent of global emissions—is far more potent in trapping heat in the atmosphere than carbon dioxide, especially over shorter periods of time, contributing enormously to global warming, which increases both the frequency and intensity of tropical storms (Romm, 2018). Warmer sea surface temperatures intensify tropical storm wind speeds, potentially delivering more damage when they make landfall. Sea-level rise, caused by global warming and the melting of the polar ice caps, is likely to make future coastal storms, including tropical storms, more damaging as well. Accordingly, anthropogenic (human-generated) global warming through the extraction, transportation, and burning of fossil fuels, including methane, for primarily socioeconomic reasons and to fuel the consumption patterns of wealthy nations is undeniably *social* in nature.

The case of Mozambique reminds us of an important paradox that we must pay serious attention to if we are to truly address the root cause of the deadly effects of tropical storms and the "climate crisis." Indeed, the so-called "climate crisis" is a *social crisis* embedded in uneven political, economic, and geographical power relations. Climate change does not affect everyone in the same way. We have already seen this in 2005 (and countless other times before and after), when Hurricane Katrina made landfall in the US Gulf South region and many Americans and people across the world witnessed a "hurricane-induced" levee failure that left residents of New Orleans inundated with flood waters. However, the devastating effects of Katrina were exacerbated by the failure of a social support system for the largely invisible inner-city poor, who were, by and large, racially black and included the elderly, women, children, and people with disabilities (Cutter, 2006). The vast majority of the Mozambican population comprises of black indigenous groups, whose marginality is rooted in colonial policies of exclusion and exploitation, resulting in economic inequality and an uneven distribution of resources and infrastructure throughout the country.

Certainly, global warming and other anthropogenic changes to the natural environment are very real and very devastating to many people's lives, but to truly solve the climate crisis requires a cultural shift in reimagining it as a social crisis, as social inequalities and inequities that exist in many parts of the world—due to colonialism, patriarchy, racism, capitalist production, and so on—are more devastating than global warming and the climate crisis itself. Yet, the so-called experts (for example, international governing bodies, climate scientists, and engineers) continue to attach the term "crisis" to climate change and to communicate that the "climate crisis" is one of the most daunting, dangerous, and defining "global issues" of our time that affects "all life" on earth, and that we must continuously find ways to protect the human species from it via mitigation and adaptation strategies. This is misleading; instead, the aftermath of Cyclones Idai and Kenneth should be attributed to the social crisis and its dominant economic associations, and this is what needs to be clearly communicated and addressed.

In the remaining part of the chapter, I focus on describing the expert approaches to climate change, including the global scientific-policy apparatus that defines and communicates dangerous climate impacts, determines climate change vulnerabilities, and informs mitigation and adaptation strategies. I then highlight some of the critiques of this so-called "expert approach," which suggest the need to reimagine the climate crisis according to the different communities that experience it as a social crisis. It is important to note that it is beyond the scope of this chapter to delve into the historical and political-economic processes and overconsumption patterns that have led to the social crisis to begin with; however, understanding these processes is, of course, integral to addressing the social crisis (see Shiva, 1993; Foster et al, 2010).

Research evidence

Established in 1982, the Intergovernmental Panel on Climate Change (IPCC)—the main body of the United Nations (UN) for assessing and communicating the science related to climate change about every five years in their major assessment reports—warns us that an increase in anthropogenic greenhouse gas emissions over the past 250 years is driving up global temperature and, in turn, altering all life on earth and accelerating species extinction. For this reason, the Paris Climate Accord was established in 2015, when 190 nations unanimously agreed to focus on *mitigation* efforts in limiting and reducing greenhouse gas emissions to a level that would avoid the worst of climate impacts, which would require keeping total global warming well below 2 °C above preindustrial levels. However, with the recent release of the IPCC's (2021) working group contributions to their *Sixth Assessment Report*—"the most up-to-date physical understanding of the climate system and climate change" (IPCC, 2021)—it is clear that even if drastic changes are made to past and present greenhouse gas emissions, global warming and climate change will continue for centuries to millennia due to the greenhouse gases that are already trapped in the atmosphere.

UN-led international climate change talks now stress the need for nations to focus on *adaptation* strategies. This entails a body of experts (for example, scientists, international policymakers, economists, and engineers) defining dangerous climate impacts, identifying vulnerable communities, and providing them with the information to adapt to these impacts. According to the IPCC (2014), the extent of dangerous climate impacts depends on the magnitude of climatic changes affecting a particular system (exposure), the characteristics of the system (sensitivity), and the ability of people and ecosystems to deal with the resulting effects (adaptive capacities of the system). These three factors determine the vulnerability of the system to climate change. Different systems, or communities, are better prepared for adaptation, in part, because of their existing vulnerabilities. As such, experts develop climate change policy measures that inform adaptation strategies targeted at specified systems, or communities.

However, Dessai et al (2004) note that these experts tend to use "top-down" approaches in defining dangerous climate impacts based on socioeconomic impacts. That is to say, they quantify indicators of vulnerability based on scenarios of future socioeconomic changes. These types of assessments typically define dangerous climate impacts, either globally or locally, in terms of physical measures (for example, affected crop yield or water availability), threats to the continued function of some part of the nonhuman world (for example, rain forests, oceans, soil, and other *carbon sinks*), or people at risk or a decline in economic welfare. Furthermore, these top-down approaches support engineering and technological advancements, which are often framed as a "sustainable" path, in both adapting to dangerous climate impacts and supporting economic growth. This leads to important questions about the ways in which the experts identify, define, communicate, and address dangerous climate impacts without focusing on understanding the dangerous *social inequality* impacts that different communities experience.

Norgaard (2018) states that we have made little progress in understanding how to actually change the course (as well as discourse) of climate change, even after four decades of "warnings" made by the IPCC. Indeed, UN-based scientific expertise is crucial to identifying human sources of climate change, clarifying biospheric effects, and informing policy to develop and implement technologies to mitigate and adapt to human-induced climate problems. However, purely relying on climate science and "technological fixes" is not sufficient enough to mitigate or effectively adapt to climate change. The so-called "climate crisis" is largely a problem of culture, social organization, power relations, and inequality. Dealing with climate change means dealing with big, complex questions about how we think and how we live in an unequal social world. As Nightingale et al (2020) note, the global scientific-policy apparatus built to tackle climate change limits our imagination and narrows the range of potential responses to climate change.

Accordingly, Norgaard (2018) and other social scientists suggest that we need to reimagine the climate crisis, which entails critiquing the dominant knowledge system that informs the social relations that make up our environmentally damaging social structures. The development of modern society rests upon the assumption that humans are separate from nature, should use nature for human well-being, and, in doing so, can control and govern it. These ideas stem from European "Enlightenment" thinking, the pursuit of "reason" and "rationality," and reliance on science and technology—all of which have helped people, particularly in modern "Western" contexts, to imagine that they can rise above nature and no longer fear or be vulnerable to it (Hulme, 2008). However, this process has led to an *ecological rift* between Western societies and nature, which has separated many people from the natural world, both physically and psychologically (Foster et al, 2010).

As such, many people in middle-class Western society rarely experience climate change. The climate crisis hardly exists to them—even as they constantly read about it in the news and worry about its potential impact—because they do not experience social inequalities on a day-to-day basis, nor do they lack adequate resources that prevents them from adapting to climate change. For example: middle-class homes are equipped with air conditioning that can mask the rise in global temperatures; food systems have been restructured so that middle-class families no longer have to worry about avocados missing from their supermarket shelves; and when a hurricane approaches their city, they have the financial resources to evacuate to a safer location before it hits. Accordingly, most people in middle-class Western society are alienated from our ecological worlds and the so-called "climate crisis" (Norgaard, 2018.

Interestingly (and not by coincidence), the powerful economic entities that contribute greatly to global warming and produce many of the world's environmentally damaging social structures—as in the case with foreign investments in the natural gas project off the coast of Mozambique—share the same dominant knowledge system as the experts that define and inform the drivers of climate change, frame global warming as a climate crisis, and create the policies that govern climate change mitigation and adaptation. To reimagine the climate crisis as a social crisis will require recognizing the complex interweaving of Western ideas about climate change as they exist within their physical and cultural settings (Hulme, 2008). Therefore, to foster socially just climate governance, we need to recognize "how the climate change issues we are trying to solve are also products of the way they are framed in the first place and the power relations they reflect" (Nightingale et al, 2020: 344). In many parts of the world, civil society can play a major role in providing "alternative" expertise in climate-related negotiations, governance, resource allocation, and adaptation processes (Eastwood, 2011).

Recommendations and solutions

From drought in Africa and India, to wildfires in North America, Siberia, and the Mediterranean, to floods in China, Europe, and the Americas, it is clear that no continent has remained untouched from climate change and that climate change is very real and devastating to many people's lives. Emphasizing and addressing the ways in which humans are catalysts to these climatic changes through the burning of fossil fuels and the destruction of our carbon sinks for socioeconomic reasons is important, but we cannot continue to discuss the climate crisis as if it is created by all people and affects everyone in the same way. Instead, we need to recognize that the climate crisis is a *social crisis* embedded in economic and ecological imperialism, and that the communities who are deprived of their resources suffer the most.

I conclude with recommendations that will help us in reimagining the climate crisis as a social crisis and in devising socially just solutions that revolve around community engagement and equitable resource allocation, through: (1) social research; (2) community-driven policy; and (3) the role of nongovernmental organizations (NGOs) and environmental justice organizations. Of course, other strategies that address economic and ecological imperialism on a broad structural and systemic scale need to be implemented, but to do this should also include the voices and perspectives of the people who actually experience social inequality and the social dilemmas of climate change.

Social research

Future social research should focus on exploring the linkages and gaps between external (expert) conceptions of dangerous climate impacts, climate change vulnerabilities, and climate change mitigation and adaptation processes, and internal (community-based) perceptions and experiences with social inequality and the social dilemmas of climate change. This research should seriously consider both analyzing the dominant knowledge systems that inform climate change governance and adaptation processes, and understanding "other" knowledge systems, which may entail "replacing vulnerability, adaptation, and mitigation as central concepts with more nuanced, plural conceptualizations of the co-emergence of societies and global climate change" (Nightingale et al, 2020: 344).

Analyzing external approaches

Research should analyze top-down approaches to addressing climate change vulnerabilities in different regions of the world. This research would require a critical analysis of the climate change discourses taken up in UN negotiations that inform and govern climate change policy. This research could also analyze how governments use this information in adopting and implementing regional and national climate change mitigation and adaptation plans. Researchers could draw upon institutional ethnography and environmental discourse analysis in understanding and critiquing these top-down strategies.

Understanding internal approaches

Research should also explore perceived, anticipated, or experienced social impacts of climate change among different communities throughout the world. This research should focus on understanding the lived experiences of various communities, that is, their shared values, social norms, and coping mechanisms, as well other approaches to social inequality and the social impacts of climate change. There is a particular need to learn about these experiences and approaches in the Global South, including among black, indigenous, and brown communities, as well as to draw upon feminist perspectives, traditional ecological knowledges (TEK), and postcolonial theory. Researchers could rely upon community-based participatory research (CBPR) methods, which would produce more diverse and inclusive conceptions in understanding the climate crisis as a social crisis.

Community-driven policy

Future policy should also be informed by civic engagement and focus on an equitable distribution of resources in helping to alleviate social inequalities. For example, the Indigenous Peoples of Africa Co-ordinating Committee (IPACC)—a network of 135 indigenous peoples' organizations in 20 African countries—helps guide national policies surrounding social and ecological resilience. Civic engagement provides opportunities for community members most affected by social inequality to create policies that can address the devastating effects of the social impacts of climate change. Specifically, these policies should focus on preventing foreign entities from investing in and accumulating resources, and instead provide communities with the resources that they deem necessary to reduce their social vulnerability to climate impacts. Indeed, climate change is more dangerous to communities when they are deprived of their resources to alleviate social inequality. Societal and health problems associated with climate change, such as rising temperatures, droughts, floods, biodiversity loss, disease, and so on, become even more dangerous for certain communities (including: black, indigenous, brown, and resource-deprived communities; women, children, and the elderly; and people with physical disabilities and mental health issues) than more privileged, white communities—even when these communities are exposed to the same climatic hazard. Community-driven policy needs to address the severe social inequalities and inequities that exist throughout many parts of the world, which, again, is more devastating than the climate crisis itself.

NGOs and environmental justice organizations

NGOs and environmental justice organizations also play a major role in how we think about and approach the climate crisis as a social crisis. These organizations often work directly within communities throughout the world, many of which are indigenous, to help them protect and preserve their natural resources from foreign, capitalist exploitation, as well as to promote their traditional ecological knowledges. These organizations can act as intermediaries between governments working on implementing socially just resource allocation and climate change policies by learning about how communities perceive and experience social inequality and climate change. Additionally, these organizations can provide spaces and opportunities for psychological and socioemotional support, including trauma resources and grief circles, in coping with the lived experiences of social inequality and climate impacts. These spaces can further serve as important public spaces for gathering public input and engaging in grassroots mobilization and environmental activism, supporting indigenous peoples as holders of environmental knowledge, and facilitating the coproduction of knowledge and storytelling about how to live harmoniously and holistically as part and parcel of the natural environment. Such NGOs include El Centro Mexicano de Derecho Ambiental, A.C. (CEMDA), which engages indigenous communities in Mexico in defending their natural resources and right to a healthy environment, and the First Nations Health Authority in Canada, which uses the Medicine Wheel, sometimes known as the Sacred Hoop, as a method for healing and balancing the mind and the earth in the face of climate change.

References

CARE (Cooperative for Assistance and Relief Everywhere) (2021) 2 years since Cyclone Idai, Mozambique has already faced an additional 3 cyclones. Press release. Available at: www.care-international.org/news/press-releases/2-years-since-cyclone-idai-and-mozambique-has-already-faced-an-additional-3-cyclones

Cutter, S. (2006) "The Geography of Social Vulnerability: Race, Class, and Catastrophe. In *Understanding Katrina: Perspectives from the Social Sciences*. New York, NY: Social Science Research Council. Available at: https://items.ssrc.org/understanding-katrina/the-geography-of-social-vulnerability-race-class-and-catastrophe/

Dessai, S.W., Adger, N., Hulme, M., Turnpenny, J., Köhler, J., and Warren, R. (2004) Defining and experiencing dangerous climate change. *Climatic Change*, 64: 11–25. Available at: https://doi.org/10.1023/B:CLIM.0000024781.48904.45

Eastwood, L. (2011) Climate change negotiations and civil society participation: shifting and contested terrain. *Theory in Action*, 4(1): 8–37. Available at: https://doi.org/10.3798/tia.1937-0237.11002

Elston, L. and Darby, M. (2020) Gas curse: Mozambique's multi-billion dollar gamble on LNG. *Climate Home News*. Available at: www.climatechangenews.com/2020/07/10/gas-curse-mozambiques-multi-billion-dollar-gamble-lng/

Foster, J.B., Clark, B., and York, R. (2010) *The Ecological Rift: Capitalism's War on the Earth*. New York, NY: Monthly Review Press. Available at: https://monthlyreview.org/product/ecological_rift/

Hulme, M. (2008) The conquering of climate: discourses of fear and their dissolution. *The Geographical Journal*, 174(1): 5–16. Available at: https://doi.org/10.1111/j.1475-4959.2008.00266.x

IPCC (Intergovernmental Panel on Climate Change) (2014) Summary for policymakers. In C.B. Field, V.R. Barros, D.J. Dokken, K.J. Mach, M.D. Mastrandrea, T.E. Bilir, M. Chatterjee, K.L. Ebi, Y.O. Estrada, R.C. Genova, B. Girma, E.S. Kissel, A.N. Levy, S. MacCracken, P.R. Mastrandrea, and L.L. White (eds) *Climate Change 2014: Impacts, Adaptation, and Vulnerability. Part A: Global and Sectoral Aspects. Contribution of Working Group II to the Fifth Assessment Report of the Intergovernmental Panel on Climate Change*. Cambridge and New York, NY: Cambridge University Press, pp. 1-32. Available at: www.ipcc.ch/site/assets/uploads/2018/02/ar5_wgII_spm_en.pdf

IPCC (2021) Summary for policymakers. In V. Masson-Delmotte, P. Zhai, A. Pirani, S.L. Connors, C. Péan, S. Berger, N. Caud, Y. Chen, L. Goldfarb, M.I. Gomis, M. Huang, K. Leitzell, E. Lonnoy, J.B.R. Matthews, T.K. Maycock, T. Waterfield, O. Yelekçi, R. Yu, and B. Zhou (eds) *Climate Change 2021: The Physical Science Basis. Contribution of Working Group I to the Sixth Assessment Report of the Intergovernmental Panel on Climate Change*. Cambridge and New York, NY: Cambridge University Press. Available at: www.ipcc.ch/report/ar6/wg1/downloads/report/IPCC_AR6_WGI_Citation.pdf

Nightingale, A.J., Eriksen, S., Taylor, M., Forsyth, T., Pelling, M., Newsham, A., Boyd, E., Brown, K., Harvey, B., Jones, L., Bezner Kerr, R., Mehta, L., Naess, L.O., Ockwell, D., Scoones, I., Tanner, T., and Whitfield, S. (2020) Beyond technical fixes: climate solutions and the great derangement. *Climate and Development*, 12(4): 343–52. Available at: https://doi.org/10.1080/17565529.2019.1624495

Norgaard, K.M. (2018) The sociological imagination in a time of climate change. *Global and Planetary Change*, 163: 171–6. Available at: https://doi.org/10.1016/j.gloplacha.2017.09.018

Romm, J. (2018) *Climate Change: What Everyone Needs to Know* (2nd edn). Oxford: Oxford University Press. Available at: https://doi.org/10.1093/wentk/9780190866112.001.0001

Shiva, V. (1993) Monocultures of the mind—understanding the threats to biological and cultural diversity. *Indian Journal of Public Administration*, 39(3): 237–48. Available at: https://doi.org/10.1177/0019556119930304

UNICEF (United Nations Children's Fund) (2019) Cyclone Idai and Kenneth cause devastation and suffering in Mozambique. Press release. Available at: www.unicef.org/mozambique/en/cyclone-idai-and-kenneth

Further reading

Clark, B. and York, R. (2005) Carbon metabolism: global capitalism, climate change, and the biospheric rift. *Theory and Society*, 34(4): 391–428. Available at: https://doi.org/10.1007/s11186-005-1993-4

Dunlap, R.E. and Brulle, R.J. (eds) (2015) *Climate Change and Society: Sociological Perspectives*. Oxford: Oxford University Press. Available at: https://doi.org/10.1093/acprof:oso/9780199356102.001.0001

Moser, S.C. (2010) Communicating climate change: history, challenges, process and future directions. *WIREs Climate Change*, 1: 31–53. Available at: https://doi.org/10.1002/wcc.11

Nisbet, M.C. (2010) Communicating climate change: why frames matter for public engagement. *Environment: Science and Policy for Sustainable Development*, 51(2): 12–23. Available at: https://doi.org/10.3200/ENVT.51.2.12-23

Wapner, P. and Elver. H. (eds) (2016) *Reimagining Climate Change*. London: Routledge. Available at: https://doi.org/10.4324/9781315671468

PART II

Reflection pieces

TWELVE

Invitation to transnational sociology

John G. Dale and Ivan Kislenko

Introduction

What does it mean to study and understand a global social problem from the perspective of global sociology? When invited to share some thoughts on this question for the 2022 Agenda for Social Justice, we realized that any perspective or direction for such problem-solving that we might articulate would first require substantial problem "dis-solving." How we frame the problem in the first place shapes how we examine and understand it. In this chapter, we revisit a common discourse in sociology that distinguishes between a "social" and a "sociological" problem. This discourse suggests that there is an inherent aspect of sociology's disciplinary logic and orientation toward representing society that leads it to question, rather than reinforce, the framing of problems deployed by administrative disciplines. Then, we challenge the underlying assumption of this argument by highlighting examples of sociology's pernicious entanglement with administrative disciplines. We reflect on two critical agendas working not only within, but also beyond certain confines of, global sociology to discuss how each frames global sociology itself as a sociological problem—one that often reproduces structural inequalities too. We then discuss what it means to frame public sociology as a global social problem from a transnational perspective and explain how doing so can contribute to greater precision in research on the complexities of, and possibilities for, social change. We suggest that such a perspective may also help identify and create networks of critical global sociologies that transcend national borders.

Ultimately, we offer not so much a *particular* global sociological approach, but rather an invitation to transnational sociology. An invitation to transnational sociology is meant to be a critical, self-reflexive shift from sociology's legacy of democratic imperialism, which, in part, has been reproduced through the discipline's penchant for methodological nationalism and methodological eurocentrism. Certain global sociological approaches have not managed to effectively escape these problems. However, bringing a transnational *perspective* to bear on our research and analysis, while necessary, is not in itself sufficient to enable this shift. How we organize the social relations of our production of sociological knowledge is equally critical. As we will see, ours is an invitation to collaborate within a transnational perspective on social problems. However, it is also an invitation to reorganize the social relations through which we produce sociological knowledge about social problems, recognizing that such problems differently and unevenly impact us, even as we are linked across communities and societies. In short, we seek to deepen the democratic production of sociological knowledge on social problems of transnational significance and consequence.

Sociology of social problems

It has been nearly 60 years since Peter Berger (1963) published *Invitation to Sociology: A Humanistic Perspective*, a classic that, for many a student of sociology, has served as an introduction to the discipline. Berger, who (with Thomas Luckmann) would publish *The Social Construction of Reality: A Treatise in the Sociology of Knowledge* only three years later (Berger and Luckmann, 1966), introduced a distinction between a "social" problem and a "sociological" problem:

> the problems that will interest the sociologist are not necessarily what other people may call "problems." The way in which public officials and newspapers (and alas, some college textbooks in sociology) speak about "social problems" serves to obscure this fact. People commonly speak of a "social problem" when something in society does not work the way it is supposed to according to the official interpretations. They then expect the sociologist to study the "problem" as they have defined it and perhaps even to come up with a "solution" that will take care of the matter to their own satisfaction. It is important, against this sort of expectation, to understand that a sociological problem is something quite different from a "social problem" in this sense.... [T]he sociological problem is not so much why some things "go wrong" from the viewpoint of the authorities and the management of the social scene, but how the whole system works in the first place, what are its presuppositions and by what means is it held together. (Berger, 1963: 36–7)

Berger trained his readers' attention on the process through which social problems are socially constructed and encouraged them to critically question how they come to be constructed as they are. In his view, the sociologist's task was to problematize (even reframe when necessary) the preidentified social problems we inherit from authorities, public opinion, or even disciplines outside of sociology, which all vie to represent the "social." His concern was to situate any issue that might be framed as a social problem within what he called a "sociological frame of reference":

> The sociologist will be driven time and again, by the very logic of his discipline, to debunk the social systems he is studying.... [T]he roots of the debunking motif in sociology are not psychological but methodological. The sociological frame of reference, with its built-in procedure of looking for levels of reality other than those given by the official interpretations of society, carries with it a logical imperative to unmask the pretentions and the propaganda by which men cloak their actions with each other. This unmasking imperative is one of the characteristics of sociology particularly at home in the temper of the modern era. (Berger, 1963: 38)

For Berger, the sociological frame of reference was not simply a psychological predisposition shared by sociologists, nor even a cognitive process that we might associate today with cultural framing, but rather a methodological orientation inherent to sociology's disciplinary logic—to reiterate, "a built-in procedure of looking for levels of reality other than those given by official interpretations of society" (Berger, 1963: 38). Describing this logic as an "unmasking imperative" would seem to imply that sociology not only seeks to identify alternative realities to officially sanctioned ones, but also that the reality it does articulate may be somehow more real.

Writing a half-century later, French sociologist Luc Boltanski makes a similar argument about sociology's disciplinary logic in his book *Mysteries and Conspiracies: Detective Stories, Spy Novels and the Making of Modern Societies*:

> Like detective fiction, and perhaps especially like spy fiction, sociology constantly tests the *reality of reality*, or, to put it another way, it challenges *apparent* reality and seeks to reach a reality that is more hidden, more profound and more *real*. It does this while also relying on the identification of enigmas or *mysteries*, that is, events or phenomena that appear to contradict reality, or at least cannot readily be integrated into the pictures generally used to give meaning to what is happening. This deconstruction of apparent reality has gone in very different directions with different authors and traditions. (Boltanski, 2014: 32, emphasis in original)

Boltanski persuasively explains how we find this deconstruction of reality expressed over the last half-century not only in works inspired by phenomenology, pragmatism, interactionism, or ethnomethodology, "in which the enterprise of *constructing* reality is central to their perspectives" (Boltanski, 2014: 33, emphasis in original), but also in sociological traditions (inspired, in particular, by positivism) that seek to sketch social reality as a whole, that is, as it *really* is. Such approaches, Boltanski (2014: 34) explains, do not initiate their analysis with individuals immersed in situations, but rather "adopt a global perspective and base their descriptions on relations among entities known as 'collective,'" that is, individuals subsumed in categories and typically explored through statistical techniques. He identifies numerous versions of this paradigm, diversely inspired by US structuralist functionalism, Marxism, and Durkheimian thought. However, Boltanski devotes particular attention to Pierre Bourdieu's (1984 [1979]) analysis in *Distinction: A Social Critique of the Judgment of Taste*, and it is in doing so that he begins to echo Berger's argument about the critical logic inherent to the sociological enterprise.

Bourdieu, he explains, differentiates between the "official" and the "unofficial," particularly the difference between the officially recognized power of certain actors (individual or collective) holding a legal mandate and the real power that other actors whose solidarity is based on different forms of connection (family ties, common economic interests, or personal bonds) surreptitiously exercise. Boltanski argues that if sociology is to operate as an autonomous science, not as an administrative extension of the state that serves merely to confirm and reproduce the state's representation of reality, it must remain able to identify and examine unsanctioned forms of social power that challenge the power, order, and reality that the state seeks to produce and maintain. We might recall that C. Wright Mill's (1959) imagery of the "cheerful robot" warned us of precisely this point. As Boltanski (2014: 34) puts it:

> The expectation has to do with the difference between sociology and administrative disciplines, and thus with the nature and importance of the added value offered by sociological description as compared to the descriptions of society that can be procured by state-sponsored agencies relying solely or primarily on officially recognized, legally defined categories and divisions.... [T]he broader sociological enterprise I am describing necessarily includes, at least potentially, a critical orientation ... since it challenges official reality and unveils a different, much more real but hidden reality.

Thus, like Berger, Boltanski suggests that there is an inherent aspect of sociology's disciplinary logic and orientation toward representing society that leads it to question, rather than reinforce, administrative disciplines.

Depictions of sociology like Berger's and Boltanski's, while immensely instructive for a sociology of social problems, may also appear to be more aspirational than actual. As sociologists Julian Go (2016), George Steinmetz (2013, 2017), and Ali Meghji (2021) have convincingly observed, throughout the discipline's emergence in the 19th and 20th centuries, sociologists also worked directly with and in support of colonial administrations, and sociological knowledge was also explicitly invoked by colonial administrations to justify their colonial policies. Significantly, such sociological "problem-solving" was not confined to the margins of the discipline. As Steinmetz (2013) documents, Britain's Colonial Social Science Research Council (CSSRC) informed the British colonial office in 1944 that its journal *The Sociological Review* would start publishing the material most valuable to understanding the colonies. Between 1944 and 1961 (shortly prior to the publication of *Invitation to Sociology*), the CSSRC substantially funded sociological research for colonial development and the British Colonial Office implemented the Devonshire system that aimed to formally train colonial military personnel and civil servants in sociology at British universities for application under colonial conditions (see Steinmetz, 2013, 2017, cited in Meghji, 2021: 18). Given these applications of sociological research, one might reasonably question the inherent critical orientation of the sociological method or enterprise.

One of the promises of global sociology is that it can help us to transcend the limitations of the discipline's penchant for what Ulrich Beck (2005: 22) has identified as "methodological nationalism." Studying social problems, such as structural inequality, within the relational confines of a single nation-state (say, the US) can blind us to the exploitative transnational relationships upon which the US has achieved its wealth, security, and rule of law relative to poorer nation-states. By constraining our field of vision to an exclusively national outlook and issues framed as domestic social problems, we risk further marginalizing the poor within our nation-state by blinding them to any significant sources of transnational solidarity and agency that might address local, national, international, and transnational obstacles generating and perpetuating inequality and poverty. To the extent that sociology does frame social problems within the constraints of methodological nationalism may therefore imply that sociology's method is less inherently critical than we often tell ourselves.

(Re)Locating "global" sociology

The term "global sociology" has multiple meanings. Wilbert Moore (1966), a former president of the American Sociological Association and student of Talcott Parsons, seems to have first introduced the term in an article titled "Global sociology: the world as a singular system," published in the *American Journal of Sociology* in 1966. It has also been invoked to refer to the study of global social systems, such as the world economy or the emerging institution of human rights norms. It is often used to refer to the study of non-Western traditions in sociological theory or even comparative research that includes all of the countries of the world as cases. Sociologist Salvatore Balbones (2017: 466) has recently suggested that the "global" in global sociology "is in the mind of the researcher, not in the objects being researched. It is fundamentally subjective and has to do with the level at which the researcher questions and presents research results."

If global sociology has helped to overcome some of the limitations of methodological nationalism, it still struggles to overcome another type of methodological constraint. Tracing the emergence of the term "global sociology" and its diverse meanings, Kislenko (2021) identifies two recent and distinct agendas within global sociology that we particularly wish to emphasize here. Neither of these agendas is reducible to global sociology per se, but each deploys distinct global sociological perspectives in making their case.

One of these agendas calls for a "decolonial sociology." There is good reason to argue that sociology as a discipline, far from being inherently in tension with administrative disciplines, has been fundamentally shaped by colonialism and imperialism. As Ali Meghji (2021: 3) has recently argued: "sociology did not 'become' colonized; rather, it was always colonial to begin with.... [S]ociology both internalized the logic of a colonial episteme, and also (re)-produced and bolstered that very episteme itself." In other words, sociology was complicit in producing and extending the idea that the colonized were inherently different from and inferior to Western colonizers. At the same time, as Colin Samson (2020: 35–7) observes in *The Colonialism of Human Rights*, colonial and settler states (like the US, Canada, and Australia) could justify themselves as liberal because they did not see colonized people as fully human and, therefore, as qualifying under the putatively universal laws protecting the rights of man.

A common narrative within revisionist histories of sociology (see, for example, Connell, 1997) is that US sociology became increasingly insular after the Second World War, largely confining its research gaze to the study of US society. At the same time, European (and especially British) sociology imported this US sociology, especially structural functionalism. Yet, this narrative fails to account for the ongoing sociological production of colonial difference that, as we have seen, British and US sociology fostered. Moreover, as both Meghji and Samson make clear, Western sociology operating within a "global" scope remains today hypocritically complicit in promoting and exporting the idea that former Western colonial and settler states (that is, liberal states espousing democracy and human rights) are best positioned to solve the problems of inequality, violent conflict, and human deprivation in the societies that they helped to reorder.

In the 1950s and 1960s, during the pinnacle of modernization theory, Arjun Appadurai (2000: 4) reminds us: "[t]heory and method were seen as naturally metropolitan, modern, and Western. The rest of the world was seen in the idiom of cases, events, examples, and test sites in relation to this stable location for the production or revision of theory." Meghji (2021: 40) describes this bifurcation in sociology as an epistemic dividing line between the West and the rest, which entails accepting, consciously or otherwise, "the idea that if one's theoretical model works on 'this side' of the line—on the Western side—then it can achieve universality." It is a mode of knowledge production that Gurminder Bhambra (2014) calls "methodological Eurocentrism." Thus, decolonizing sociology—which both Meghji and Samson argue is still possible—relies upon a global sociological perspective. However, it does so while also critiquing a good deal of what passes for global sociological practice and acknowledging that, in itself, global sociology is necessary yet insufficient to decolonize sociology.

Public sociology as a global social problem

A second agenda influencing and influenced by global sociology calls for more "public sociology" (Sorokin, 2016; Kislenko, 2021). This agenda was largely initiated by Michael Burawoy's 2004 American Sociological Association Presidential Address, "For public sociology," published in the *American Sociological Review* (Burawoy, 2005), and has spawned vigorous debate within and outside the US. Here, we wish only to draw attention to the conditions of possibility for the democratization of research about globalization in the context of sociological knowledge production, especially as it has been organized in the West. Burawoy never intended his call for public sociology to be a US global export, nor one more Western project of democratic imperialism. However, he did intend that it might contribute to a more democratic production of sociological knowledge that might countervail the institutionalization of neoliberal global development and authoritarian state practices, both within and beyond the US. As he states in "Thesis IX" ("Provincializing American sociology") in his presidential address:

> Without conspiracy or deliberation on the part of its practitioners, United States sociology becomes world hegemonic. We, therefore, have a special responsibility to provincialize our own sociology, to bring it down from the pedestal of universality and recognize its distinctive character and national power. We have to develop a dialogue, once again, with other national sociologies, recognizing their local traditions or their aspirations to indigenize sociology. We have to think in global terms, to recognize the emergent global division of sociological labor....

> We have to encourage networks of critical sociologies that transcend not just disciplines but also national boundaries. We should apply our sociology to ourselves and become more conscious of the global forces that are driving our discipline, so that we may channel them rather than be channeled by them. (Burawoy, 2005: 22)

In a telling article, "Can 'public sociology' travel as far as Russia?"—the product of a talk and discussion at the Center for Independent Social Research in St. Petersburg three years after his presidential address—Burawoy (2009: 203, emphasis in original) raises an additional "deeper issue": "Can there be a public sociology without genuine publics? We need to think through a sociology *of* publics before we can have a sociology *for* publics."

But what might such a sociology of "publics" entail? Are we to imagine "national" publics, or would such a conception include counterpublics (Warner, 2005) who might imagine themselves (and as perhaps we should imagine them) as transnational social formations? How precisely should we "think in global terms"? As we map an emergent global division of sociological labor, should we be mapping the production of sociological knowledge within siloed national boundaries for comparative purposes, laying the groundwork for dialogue with other national sociologies? We think that this risks reproducing sociological thinking about justice, law, and power as operating exclusively within the confines of a hegemonic international system of nation-states, thereby blinding us to the optics of a transnational legal pluralism that often provides social actors with alternative notions of justice and sources of power (Dale and Samara, 2008; Berman, 2012). We embrace the spirit of Burawoy's message in this address, but we also perceive in this discourse a corollarial form of methodological nationalism that is shaped by global–local binary thinking.

In the prevailing discourse on "globalization," "global" and "local" social processes have been framed in binary opposition, that is, as mutually exclusive and inherently antagonistic explanations for urban and legal development, affecting how we apply our sociology to ourselves. We have learned especially from urban and legal research and analysis in sociology and anthropology (Smith, 2001; Goodale and Merry, 2007) that the global–local binary frame has been conflated with the economic–cultural and universal–particular dichotomies. The effect is that we are left with no conceptual space for analyzing the transnationally situated actors, relations, practices, and agency that most often shape the complexities of, and possibilities for, social change.

If we are to not only encourage, but also engage and understand with any precision, networks of critical sociologies that transcend national borders, as Burawoy suggests, then we will be required to think not only globally, but also transnationally. As Michael Peter Smith (2002: 3–4, emphasis in original) observes: "[u]nlike the globalization discourse ... theorists of transnationalism tend to treat the nation-state and transnational practices as mutually *constitutive* rather than mutually exclusive social formations." If the globalization discourse trains our attention on social processes that are largely decentered from specific national territories, research on transnational processes sees transnational social relations and formations as anchored in, while also transcending, one or more nation-states.

Whose global social problem? Democratic production of sociological knowledge

However, bringing a transnational "perspective" to bear on our research and analysis, while necessary, is not sufficient to enable a shift in US sociology becoming less "world hegemonic" and more "provincial." A global sociological perspective for framing global (or transnational) social problems, we have suggested, should vigilantly defend against methodological Eurocentrism and methodological nationalism, including global–local binary thinking, if it is to critically challenge official hegemonic discourses on the reality of globalization. As cultural structures, we find these concepts analytically useful for framing and critically challenging globalization as a sociological problem. For example, we might frame public sociology as a type of sociological knowledge embedded and produced within unequal transnational relations of power that partially constitute, and are partially constituted by, a transnational capitalist knowledge economy that is also, yet differently, socially organized to accelerate social inequality within and between networks, cultures, societies, institutions, and publics.

As normative guidelines, however, they undoubtedly will meet with a mixed reception, depending on the publics they address. The deeper challenge we see in collectively constructing both a sociology "of" publics and a sociology "for" publics is how we transnationally and democratically reorganize and institutionalize the unequal social relations of our production of sociological knowledge about globalization and its uneven development and impact on our experience. If we, in the US or in the "West," are prepared to move beyond a model of internationalizing sociological research that is mainly concerned with how others practice "our" precepts (and it is not clear that there is shared consensus about these precepts even within the US), then we must also be open to learning how to formulate research problems together by rethinking: the research ethics by which we judge and regulate sociological competency; the values we have ensconced within institutional review boards; the norms of ownership regarding data and intellectual property; the languages and styles of writing, publishing, and otherwise disseminating knowledge; how we fund, control, and share resources; how we organize our relations with our research subjects; how we collaborate in knowledge production with organizations and movements outside the academy; how we construct and evaluate theory together; and so much more. Yet, deliberating and negotiating all of this on an uneven playing field will likely bias the endeavor toward internationalizing our own model. That is how hegemonic inequality works.

Our invitation to transnational sociology seeks more than a change in perspective on social problems. We seek to deepen the democratic production of sociological knowledge on social problems of transnational significance and consequence. This entails collaborative, transnational, democratic experimentation and learning, with an aim toward developing and deploying research, theories, and strategies to deepen democracy in formal politics, the economy, and civil society, all of which are critical to democratizing the transnational production of sociological knowledge—including knowledge for democratizing globalization.

References

Appadurai, A. (2000) Grassroots globalization and the research imagination. *Public Culture*, 12(1): 1–19. Available at: https://doi.org/10.1215/08992363-12-1-1

Balbones, S. (2017) Global sociology. In K. Korgen (ed) *The Cambridge Handbook of Sociology: Core Areas in Sociology and the Development of the Discipline*. Cambridge: Cambridge University Press pp 465–74.

Beck, U. (2005) *Power in the Global Age: A New Global Political Economy*. Cambridge: Polity.

Berger, P.L. (1963) *Invitation to Sociology: A Humanistic Perspective*. Garden City, NY: Anchor Books.

Berger, P.L. and Luckmann, T. (1966) *The Social Construction of Reality: A Treatise in the Sociology of Knowledge*. Garden City, NY: Anchor Books.

Berman, P.S. (2012) *Global Legal Pluralism: A Jurisprudence of Law Beyond Borders*. New York, NY: Cambridge University Press.

Bhambra, G.K. (2014) *Connected Sociologies*. London: Bloomsbury.

Boltanski, L. (2014) *Mysteries and Conspiracies: Detective Stories, Spy Novels and the Making of Modern Societies*. Cambridge: Polity.

Bourdieu, P. (1984 [1979]) *Distinction: A Social Critique of the Judgment of Taste*. Cambridge, MA: Harvard University Press.

Burawoy, M. (2005) For public sociology. *American Sociological Review*, 70(1): 4–28. Available at: https://doi.org/10.1177/000312240507000102

Burawoy, M. (2009) Can "public sociology" travel as far as Russia? *Laboratorium: Russian Review of Social Research*, 1(1): 197–204.

Connell, Raewyn. (1997) Why is classical theory classical? *American Journal of Sociology* 102(6): 1511-57.

Dale, J.G. and Samara, T.R. (2008) Legal pluralism within a transnational network of governance: the extraordinary case of rendition. *Law, Social Justice & Global Development Journal*, 2. Available at: https://warwick.ac.uk/fac/soc/law/elj/lgd/2008_2/daleandsamara/

Go, J. (2016) *Postcolonial Thought and Social Theory*. New York, NY: Oxford University Press.

Goodale, M. and Merry, S.E. (eds) (2007) *The Practice of Human Rights: Tracking Law between the Global and the Local*. Cambridge: Cambridge University Press.

Kislenko, I. (2021) Debates on global sociology: unity and diversity of interpretations. *The American Sociologist*, 52(3): 579–90. Available at: doi: 10.1007/s12108-021-09478-0

Meghji, A. (2021) *Decolonizing Sociology: An Introduction*. Cambridge: Polity.

Mills, C.W. (1959) *The Sociological Imagination*. New York, NY: Oxford University Press.

Moore, W.E. (1966) Global sociology: the world as a singular system. *American Journal of Sociology*, 71(5): 475–82. Available at: https://doi.org/10.1086/224165

Samson, C. (2020) *The Colonialism of Human Rights: Ongoing Hypocrisies of Western Liberalism*. Cambridge: Polity.

Smith, M.P. (2001) *Transnational Urbanism: Locating Globalization*. Oxford: Blackwell Publishers.

Sorokin, P. (2016) "Global sociology" in different disciplinary practices: current conditions, problems, and perspectives. *Current Sociology*, 64(1): 41–59.

Steinmetz, G. (2013) A child of the Empire: British sociology and colonialism, 1940s–1960s. *Journal of the History of Behavioral Sciences*, 49(4): 353–78. Available at: https://doi.org/10.1002/jhbs.21628

Steinmetz, G. (2017) Sociology and colonialism in the British and French empires, 1945–1965. *The Journal of Modern History*, 89(3): 601–48.

Warner, M. (2005) *Publics and Counterpublics*. Brooklyn, NY: Zone Books.

THIRTEEN

Global social justice research, teaching, and activism: a global turn in sociology?

Jerry A. Jacobs and Elinore Avni

The opportunity

Today's most compelling social problems require global solutions. While this claim is not entirely new, we suggest that a series of recent developments may make a global perspective increasingly salient. The COVID-19 pandemic, the ever-more-pressing threats posed by climate change, and the need to address issues of racial justice have propelled global issues to a new level of common-sense understanding. As Karl Mannheim (1970) suggested, historical events can shape the experience and perspective of generations. We feel that the combination of the pandemic, climate change, and Black Lives Matter may coalesce to shape the future of sociology. This may well be a moment in which there is a turn toward issues of global social justice, not just for one segment of sociologists, but for the discipline as whole. In this chapter, we argue for more attention to global issues in terms of research, teaching, and activism.

The global COVID-19 pandemic that began in 2020 showed that some social issues are irreducibly global in scope. New waves of COVID-19 break out in localities and countries around the world as our global economic and social system makes it exceedingly difficult to cordon off nations, even geographically isolated places, such as New Zealand.

The pandemic also demonstrated the power of international scientific cooperation in compelling new ways: biomedical scientists have collaborated with remarkable speed across national borders; detailed genetic analyses revealed the direction of international flows of the infection; scientists shared data on genome sequences; international consortia collaborated on vaccine research; and clinical vaccine trials enrolled patients from multiple countries. The rapid advances in vaccines and treatments have, in turn, highlighted the need for a global system of producing and disseminating these vital tools.

The pandemic has shown that science and international cooperation are indispensable in this kind of crisis; yet, paradoxically, the COVID-19 crisis has also led to a backlash against both global cooperation and science. The effort to blame China for the virus, the intensified barriers to immigration, and the extensive resistance to scientific advice are just three indicators that international science is being challenged just as it is most needed.

Surveys report that many Americans are ill-informed regarding international issues (Council on Foreign Relations, 2019). There is thus much work to be done to bring our students and the broader public to understand the social world outside the borders of the US and to appreciate the global dimensions of issues of social justice.

Unfortunately, as a global scholarly discipline, sociology lags far behind the biomedical sciences in its capacity for large-scale, rapid-fire international collaborative research. While the pandemic raises countless issues about the state of our society and the challenges we need to address going forward, as a discipline, sociology is not well positioned to respond in a timely way to the challenges posed by the COVID-19 pandemic. Moreover, as a distinct field of inquiry, sociology is relatively well developed in certain countries but is quite weak and not entirely independent of state control in others.

Globalizing sociological research

Global sociology has deep roots in the discipline, as the founding figures in the field took the entirety of human experience as their purview. Moreover, many scholars have conducted important research and developed powerful theories about global inequalities. Notable lines of inquiry include world systems theory, studies of anticolonial social movements, and analyses of racism and sexism as global systems of inequality, among many others. Yet, despite the existence of these lines of inquiry, the majority of research by sociologists at US institutions of higher education focuses on the US. The principal journals are almost all in one language (English), disproportionately concentrated in the US, and typically focus on US topics using US data.

Over the years, the charge of "ethnocentrism" in US sociology has been raised by a variety of authors. The dominant position of the US, in turn, affects sociological research worldwide. We find it particularly troubling that most research that focuses on social problems and issues of social justice fit the pattern of US-focused scholarship. Our study of research published in the journal *Social Problems*—the main scholarly publication of the progressive Society for the Study of Social Problems—reveals that even in this journal, the overwhelming preponderance of research published draws on data from the US (Jacobs and Avni, 2021). The great majority of authors of articles published in *Social Problems* obtained their bachelor's or doctoral degrees in the US. It is clear that both substance and authorship skews toward the US. Articles published in *Social Problems* were more US-focused than were the other two leading sociological journals: the *American Sociological Review* and the *American Journal of Sociology* (Jacobs and Mizrachi, 2020; for similar conclusions, see also Kurien, 2016; Lie, 1995; Kurzman, 2017; Smith, 2017). In short, we see a need to greatly expand globally oriented sociological research and scholarship in US journals and by American authors.

Globalizing teaching

In additional to making globally oriented research more central to the discipline, we also believe that there is much to be done to make undergraduate teaching more global in scope. Most of the topics covered in social problems textbooks used in US colleges and universities are examined in the US context. In general, social issues are approached from a US vantage point, though the authors sometimes note that these issues are not unique to the US. Globalization and global inequality are not routinely featured as separate chapters.

Notable exceptions to these generalizations include Anna Leon-Guerrero's (2019) *Social Problems: Community, Policy and Social Action* and A. Javier Treviño's (2021) *Investigating Social Problems*, as each offers an international section in each chapter. Robin Cohen and Paul Kennedy's (2013) *Global Sociology* is still more inclusive in its orientation. Students who read these books will recognize that there is much to be learned from considering how social problems are defined and addressed in countries other than the US.

Along with the pandemic, we see climate change as a potent opportunity for introducing global themes in undergraduate classes. Climate change remains a fundamental and growing threat, and international cooperation in the development and collection of routine climate indicators is an essential input into the decision-making processes surrounding this set of issues (Fankhauser, 2020). However, climate change has not yet become a standard chapter in US social problems textbooks.

Activism

The remarkable international diffusion of Black Lives Matter protests represents a third potentially game-changing development. In response to the video of the death of George Floyd at the hands of police in Minneapolis, marches quickly spread across major cities not only in the US, but also around the world. This was, of course, not the first case in which brutal inhumanity had been exposed. Organizations such as Amnesty International work diligently to monitor human rights issues throughout the world. And it was not the first case in which demands for the protection of human rights became a truly global concern. At the present moment, the expulsion of the Rohingya from Myanmar, the concentration camps for Uyghurs in China, the plight of displaced Syrians, and the Venezuelan diaspora have all garnered international attention, though none on the scale of the Black Lives Matter movement. It is rare for even the most outrageous cases of injustice to garner international interest to the extent that occurred in May and June of 2020 (Daragahi, 2020).

Recommendations and solutions

We believe that a call for a "global turn" in sociology is needed. The multiple global crises facing the world today make it possible that researchers, scholars, and a new generation entering academia may be responsive to this call. To expand the focus on global social justice research, teaching, and activism, we need to recognize the obstacles that inhere in the current structure of rewards in academia. We believe that there is no single, silver-bullet solution to the issues raised here; thus, a multifaceted strategy should be pursued. We divide solutions into three main components: (1) making the case; (2) increasing visibility and recognition; and (3) increasing capacity.

Making the case

The strategy for increasing the focus on global social justice issues begins with making the case on intellectual terms. There are many researchers who have flexibility in the topics they investigate; thus, expanding the number of research studies conducted in this area naturally begins by making an intellectually compelling case that social justice issues are best understood in a global context and that a global perspective can help to contribute to effective long-term solutions.

The examples of the pandemic, climate change, and Black Lives Matter can easily be defined in global terms, though many individuals still view these topics in local or national terms. We suggest that using these inherently global cases as starting points may be a good way to make a broader case for studying social justice in a global context:

- The first way to broaden these cases is by using them to highlight the structural inequalities in our national and international systems. For example, COVID-19 has highlighted health disparities in both the US and other countries. Marginalized communities bore the brunt of the pandemic. As the vaccines became available, the pandemic exposed the inequalities in our global health and pharmaceutical systems. Dramatic disparities between rich and poor countries in the accessibility of vaccines and in the capacity to distribute these to large populations also became evident. Thus, the structural and systemic inequalities revealed by the pandemic can serve as a point of entry into an understanding of global health inequalities, as well as global inequalities more generally. Similar points can be made with respect to climate change and the mobilizations against racial injustice.

- A second strategy might build on these examples as emblematic cases. In other words, global issues like inequality, violence against women, racism, refugees, and so on all share some of the same defining features as the pandemic. While each of these issues is often refracted through a local or national prism, the fact is that we live in an interconnected world, and it is not just viruses and greenhouse gasses that traverse national boundaries. Ideas, cultural tropes, economic models, and political forces are global in scope; thus, issues of social justice have an international, as well as a national and regional, dimension.
- A third strategy emphasizes the value of comparative policy analyses. A comparative approach, while recognizing global influences and constraints, could point to particular policy choices that are not fully determined by the world system. Again, the pandemic and climate change provide many examples of some countries acting more boldly and effectively than others. A comparative approach can thus complement a global perspective by highlighting the role of local agency. This comparative policy focus often characterizes cross-national studies of education, healthcare, and other social policies.
- Finally, even for researchers who are not focused on issues of social justice, there is a strong case to be made for the value of comparative international research. In other words, social science knowledge is more likely to be generalizable when conclusions are based on studies of multiple countries. An exclusive focus on the US case (or on cases within the US, such as the city of Chicago) risks generalizing from a single and perhaps idiosyncratic case.

Increasing recognition and visibility

In addition to making the case for global social justice research, we can try to increase the visibility of, and recognition for, the important research that has already been conducted. In other words, it is important to remember that the call for more global social justice research does not start from scratch. There is a long history of globally oriented research, and there are a number of important organizations and conferences that can help to sound the call for more attention to this important area of research and scholarship.

We feel that it is important to emphasize the significant organizational efforts to promote international research and scholarship of the Society for the Study of Social Problems (SSSP), the American Sociological Association (ASA), and the International Sociological Association (ISA) (Patel, 2009). The Global Division of the SSSP has been active since 2005 in examining "global and transnational processes [that] both intensify and mitigate existing social problems as well as contribute to the generation of new ones" (Society for the Study of Social Problems, 2022). Likewise, the Global and Transnational Sociology Section of the ASA serves as an organization hub for research and activism on these issues. Moreover, the ASA Section on the Political Economy of the World System must surely be mentioned in this context.

While there is no research committee (RC) of the ISA that is devoted to "social problems" *per se*, many of the ISA RCs focus on issues of interest to social problems scholars. For example, ISA RC 19 focuses on "poverty, social welfare, and social policy," while ISA RC 48 focuses on "social movements, collective action, and social change." The goal of strengthening an international focus on social problems is thus not a matter of starting from square one, but rather one of building on intellectual capacity and organizational structures that are already in place.

Yet, there is much that can and should be done to strengthen the efforts of these leaders in the field. Strengthening the coverage of issues of global social justice in review essays in the *Annual Review of Sociology* and in textbooks for courses on social problems would help to raise the visibility of research in this area.

Expanding resources

Global social justice research can be difficult, expensive, and time-consuming. Launching a major initiative in this area will require considerable resources. We divide resources into the five categories of funding, infrastructure, coordination and cooperation, faculty and students, and publication outlets:

- Additional funding for global social justice research will be needed. While it can be expensive to conduct high-quality research in one venue, doing so on a global scale will be even more challenging. Foundations as well as national sources of funding are likely to be the principal sources of support for research and scholarship.
- Research on a number of topics is facilitated by the establishment of national data-collection systems. These data-collection systems can be viewed as part of a global research infrastructure. Researchers can draw on these data sources and can build on them. For example, much of the research on the pandemic has been based on data-collection systems that were in place in advance of the crisis. While state institutions routinely gather data on economic, criminal justice, education, and vital statistics, the institutional capacity to field original sociological research is not as extensive as one might hope for. A broader and more comprehensive system of data collection on global social justice issues—including

quantitative, qualitative, and social-media data—would go a long way to advancing our understanding of these issues.

- Developing a system to facilitate international collaborations will no doubt be an indispensable part of a truly global research effort. High-quality research requires extensive local knowledge. Just to take a simple example, a survey must be translated into many languages in order to make it truly international in scope, and many subtleties and nuances are easily lost without expert native-language collaboration. An international system, perhaps based in the ISA, should be developed to promote cross-national collaborative research. Such networks can build on each other so that, over time, it may become easier to find international research partners.

- Among the scarce resources for global social justice research is a critical mass of researchers and scholars working on these issues. Recent research has reported that internationally oriented appointments in US sociology departments are the exception (Stevens et al., 2018). Expanding the number of faculty hires is likely to be needed. In the long run, expanding capacity in this area will involve recruiting a new generation of students who recognize the importance of approaching social justice issues from a comparative and global framework.

- In terms of publication outlets, we should seek to increase the representation of international research in top journals, as well as to expand the outlets and visibility of journals oriented to international social justice issues. While a number of journals focus on comparative research on particular topics, such as education and healthcare, journals that focus on global social justice remain scarce. While there should be efforts to increase the representation of global issues in the top journals, a new journal called *International Social Problems* might encourage researchers to target this area for their scholarship.

Conclusion

In this chapter, we have made the case for bolstering a global focus on social justice in terms of research, teaching, and activism. We suggest that the COVID-19 pandemic of 2020, the increasing centrality of climate change, and the renewed focus on issues of racial justice have elevated the importance of approaching social problems from an international perspective. In the US, research, teaching, and activism have all emphasized US social issues.

We propose a multipronged effort to expand global social justice research. The strands of this effort include making the case for expanded research and scholarship in this area, enhancing the recognition and visibility of extant research and scholarship, and considerably expanding the resources needed to conduct high-quality international scholarship on issues of global social justice. We similarly argue for more global emphasis in teaching and activism.

Since its inception in the 19th century, sociology has endeavored to understand the modern experience and to improve the condition of contemporary societies. We maintain here that these twin goals can be promoted by expanding the scope of social problems research beyond the US experience and drawing more fully on the struggles and models offered by other societies around the world. The increasingly global nature of social issues and social movements speaks to the importance of greatly expanding our capacity to conduct global-oriented social problems research and scholarship. We hope that the readers of this volume on global social justice will help to lead this undertaking.

References

Cohen, R. and Kennedy, P. (2013) *Global Sociology* (3rd edn). New York, NY: New York University Press.

Council on Foreign Relations (2019) Americans lack knowledge of international issues yet consider them important, new survey finds. Available at: www.cfr.org/news-releases/americans-lack-knowledge-international-issues-yet-consider-them-important-finds-new

Daragahi, G. (2020) Why the Geoge Floyd protest went global. *Atlantic Council.* Available at: https://www.atlanticcouncil.org/blogs/new-atlanticist/george-floyd-protests-world-racism/

Fankhauser, S. (2020) Why we need more social science research on climate change. Grantham Research Institute on Climate Change and the Environment. Available at: https://www.lse.ac.uk/GranthamInstitute/news/why-we-need-more-social-science-research-on-climate-change/

Jacobs, J.A. and Avni, E. (2021) A global turn in sociology: approaching social problems from an international vantage point. Working paper, Population Studies Center, University of Pennsylvania. Available at: https://repository.upenn.edu/cgi/viewcontent.cgi?article=1076&context=psc_publications

Jacobs, J.A. and Mizrachi, N. (2020) International representation in US social-science journals. *American Sociologist*, 51(2): 215–39.

Kurien, P. (2016) Sociology in America or a sociology of America? Navigating American academia as an "international" scholar. Isa.e-Forum. Available at: https://www.researchgate.net/profile/Prema_Kurien/publication/311570839Sociology_in_America_or_a_Sociology_of_America/links/584d76dc08aeb9892525a182/Sociology-in-America-or-a-Sociology-of-America.pdf

Kurzman, C. (2017) Scholarly attention and the limited internationalization of U.S. social science. *International Sociology*, 32(6): 775–95.

Leon-Guerrero, A. (2019) *Social Problems: Community, Policy and Social Action* (6th edn). Los Angeles, CA: Pine Forge Press (Sage Publications).

Lie, J. (1995) American sociology in a transnational world: against parochialism. *Teaching Sociology*, 23(2): 136–44.

Mannheim, K. (1970) The problem of generations. *Psychoanalytic Review*, 57: 378–404.

Patel, Sujata, (ed) (2009) *ISA Handbook of Diverse Sociological Traditions*. Los Angeles, CA: Sage.

Smith, D.A. (2017) Globalizing social problems: an agenda for the twenty-first century. *Social Problems*, 64: 1–13.

Society for the Study of Social Problems (2022) Global Division. Available at: https://www.sssp1.org/index.cfm/pageid/1239/m/464

Stevens, M., Idriss-Miller, C., and Shami, S. (2018) *Seeing the World: How Universities Make Knowledge in a Global Era*. Princeton, NJ: Princeton University Press.

Treviño, A.J. (2021) *Investigating Social Problems*. Newbury Park, CA: Sage Publications.

FOURTEEN

A sociology of hope: why we need a radical action agenda for social justice

Corey Dolgon

From the Dust
From the mud
From the fields
The voices will rise
The voices of challenge.

Do not rest easy, do not be deceived
Those who have suffered and died
Those who have sacrificed for freedom
Their voices will challenge you
Endlessly, until we are free.

Dennis Brutus

In April 2013, Canadian Prime Minister Stephen Harper responded to questioning about a thwarted terrorist attack by claiming: "It's time to treat these things as serious threats…. this is not a time to commit sociology" (*National Post*, 2013). At the time, he and then-candidate Justin Trudeau had debated the merits of looking for *root causes* to social problems. Instead, Harper held fast to his administration's focus on punishing more criminals with harsher sentences to stop crime. His colleague, Conservative MP Pierre Poilievre, doubled down on Harper's anti-intellectualism, suggesting that while there is nothing necessarily wrong with trying to understand why terrorism happens, he deduced, "The root cause of terrorism is terrorists" (Fitzpatrick, 2013).

Just over a year later, Harper would reiterate his "penal populism" (Pratt, 2007) in the case of a murdered Native Canadian teen, Tina Fontaine. Despite the demand of Canadian First Nations for a federal inquiry into the disappearance of over 1,100 aboriginal women, Harper insisted that these were each individual criminal cases, not a "sociological phenomenon." As social scientist and nongovernmental organization (NGO) activist Craig Jones (2015) explained, penal populism represents:

[the right-wing] politicization of criminal justice and drug policy for short-term electoral advantage combined with a sympathetic— but largely content-free—discourse about "victims" amounting to a degradation of our justice system…. [It is] characterized by open hostility toward evidence, disdain for harm reduction, and contempt for science, and disinterest in what works to limit the damage from incarceration, drug prohibition and drug use.

Harper and his Conservative Party were roundly criticized, and sociologists had one of those rare opportunities to explain just how important committing sociology really was. Books and articles flipped the script on the phrase, proudly fronting *Committing Sociology* as the title to their works (Matthews, 2014; Doucet and Siltanen, 2017; Knudson and Hahn, 2020). Meanwhile, sociology bloggers and essayists used Harper's nonsense as an opportunity to uplift the discipline's effective ideological critique of what Robert Bellah (2007) once called "hyper individualism." As one blogger wrote: "Our cultural individualism blinds us from understanding the root causes of our problems and prevents us from getting beyond individual responsibility to an understanding of social accountability and political responsibility" (Wynn, 2013; see also Brym and Ramos, 2013; August, 2014). By not committing sociology, we fail to address the root causes of social problems, thus protecting "the entrenched interests of wealth that have built institutions to protect, rationalize, and justify their advantages as normal, just, and fair" (*The Sociological Post*, 2020).

In the Society for the Study of Social Problems' (SSSP's) teaching sociology newsletter—*The Baddass Sociologist*—I described committing sociology as that act of challenging "students and communities and institutions and societies to peel back the veneer of common sense and simple platitudes" (Dolgon, 2013). To critique the idea that personal responsibility was at the foundation of social problems, I argued, "We could no better stop terrorism by killing all the terrorists than we could stop crime by locking up all the 'criminals,' understand poverty by blaming poor people, or solve environmental degradation by killing the grass and trees" (Dolgon, 2013). Instead, I proposed that "Teaching sociology, especially a sociology focused on social problems, will and perhaps should be a dangerous act" (Dolgon, 2013), and the increasing use of engaged research and pedagogy could help us encourage students and colleagues to act directly and effectively for social justice on their campuses and surrounding communities.

Examining this excellent collection of scholars and activists committing sociology in the *Global Agenda for Social Justice 2*, I am somewhat heartened by my colleagues' keen eyes on the contours of global social problems, as well as their innovative instincts toward proposals for change. From school segregation to climate change, from water security and struggling single mothers to migration and pandemic-related public health inequalities, these chapters outline the dynamics of oppression, discrimination, and exploitation, while suggesting potential policies and practices that might ameliorate them. Such work has traditionally been the bedrock of committing sociology.

However, it seems to me that we must enter a new phase of engaging a more radical and practical sense of what it means to "commit sociology." Despite the successful critique of penal populism (Newburn and Jones, 2005; Pratt, 2007), the individualistic approach to social problems still saturates our academic disciplines, political discourse, and public policies. Despite troves of educational research demonstrating the resources necessary for successful teaching and learning, we continue to cut public education budgets and implement high-stakes testing to measure poorly designed outcomes for both faculty and students. Despite myriad evidence from public health research on nutrition and youth development, we persist in subsidizing fast food and lack the financial commitments necessary to provide safe and clean environments and programs for youth activities, especially in poor rural and urban areas. Despite the continued research on the apocalyptic results of economic austerity and privatization strategies, cutting dollars and outsourcing everything remains de rigueur (Dolgon, 2015). In other words, no matter how good, how clever, and how clear we commit sociology to research and analyze what is good and what is bad for people, the last few decades have produced: a world more susceptible to climate devastation and pandemics; the degradation of women's rights; the corporatization of food, medicine, and education; the rise of authoritarian regimes; and the decline of whatever one "might" have thought civilization was or could be. After all, even Gandhi supposedly thought Western civilization would be a good idea—he just knew that up until the mid-20th century, it had been mostly a brutal system of racist exploitation and global theft. It has not gotten all that much better in the last century, and in some ways, it is much worse.

In response to the "gap" or "disconnect" between academic scholarship—research, analysis, and ideological critique—and the practical policies and politics of contemporary US society, many professional organizations have examined ways to empower their scholars to be more publicly accessible and engaged. Training seminars and tool kits on "how to write an editorial" or produce a podcast have inspired researchers to reconsider how they communicate beyond the classroom and the pages of professional journals. A very insightful publication sponsored by the National Science Foundation and produced by the American Sociological Association, entitled "A relational model for understanding the use of research in the policy process" (Spalter-Roth et al, 2018), shows how sociological analysis can be employed to understand the knowledge production and diffusion process and to strategize about best practices for public impact. It is not impossible to demonstrate effectively why committing sociology matters and how to apply our work to real-life situations. Still, the disconnect continues and the gap widens.

I think the crux of the problem can be found in a 2006 *New York Times* op-ed by Harvard sociologist Orlando Paterson. (Apparently, *he* does not have that much trouble getting his work into the popular media.) Patterson blamed sociologists themselves for their irrelevancy, though not because they did not know how to write editorials or talk to legislators. Instead, he cited a "deep-seated dogma" that emphasized structural over cultural causation. For example, Patterson argued that sociologists too often found low incomes, joblessness, poor schools, and bad housing as causes for poverty. Patterson declared that subcultural group values, beliefs, and attitudes proved *more* determinative, and sociologists had to stop ignoring culture to explain persistent poverty and racial inequality.

Patterson is wrong about so many things that it is hard to spend adequate time on each error. First, sociologists had *not* ignored culture at all. Lawrence Mead, Charles Murray, and George Gilder, for example, comprised the social science front line of the Reagan administration's welfare state decimation. These scholars claimed that cultural deficits caused persistent poverty among nonwhite populations. Despite their shoddy, racist, and ultimately disproven arguments, they received great attention and entrée into the halls of power and policymaking as conservative politicians and pundits found ideological cover for dismantling progressive social policy. Maybe Patterson was only half-wrong—forsaking structural for cultural causation *does* buy you influence and public notoriety as a sociologist, not because your work provides better analyses, but because it aligns so neatly with white supremacy and corporate hegemony. Thus, even *if* sociologists learn how to speak the language of editors, policy bureaus, and elected officials, committing sociology for social justice will continue to be marginalized by the institutional and foundational power of wealth and whiteness. Committing sociology for social justice may never be popular with, or even welcomed by, those who control government, corporations, or the media.

Most notably, though, Patterson makes the same mistake that the history of colonized sociology has made: only nonwealthy and nonwhite people seem to even have "culture." For example, Patterson echoes Lawrence Mead in assuming the inherent virtue of Western values like individualism, entrepreneurialism, and a "certain moral temperament" that resulted in success for so many native and European white Americans. However, as my colleague Timothy Black and I suggested about Mead:

> [He] produces no evidence to substantiate his western versus
> nonwestern cultural orientation theory. He simply presents a tautology
> that the persistence of "serious poverty" is evidence enough to attribute
> economic outcomes to the historical and cultural origins of nonwhite

populations. Unsurprisingly, he does not try to prove the origins of individualistic entrepreneurialism in the corruption of the medieval Catholic Church or in Luther's reactionary asceticism. Nor does he try to locate the human virtue of social democracy in Britain's barbaric imperialism in Asia or in Belgium's ruthless colonialism in the Congo or French atrocities in Algeria. A more comprehensive examination of history shows that the very "western civilization" Mead premises his theory with was advanced on the bodies of black, brown, and native peoples by brute force and greed, not some superior morality. (Black and Dolgon, 2021: 509)

Patterson's claim that the cultural deficits of young black men "keep them from success" simply reaffirms the normalcy of existing power relations and structures. Such perspectives give ideological cover to the entrenched and institutionalized power of wealth. As Walter Benjamin (1986) once surmised: "There is no document of civilization which is not at the same time a document of barbarism." Traditional social science, as a production of settler-colonial universities and white corporate arrogance, has provided the morality and rationality for that continued barbaric disposition. All of this is to say that even social justice-oriented sociology is subject to the limitations of liberal premises, elite knowledge production, white supremacy, and corporate hegemony.

Recent calls to "decolonize universities," and to decolonize sociology in particular, hold great promise to inspire a more radical sociology adept at using the discipline to create more fundamental social change. By relocating the foundations of sociology in the work of W.E.B. Dubois, Jane Addams, Ida B. Wells, and others, recent academics have challenged the discipline's origin stories entrenched in the Chicago School's racist theoretical and methodological approaches. The contours of so much contemporary sociology still remain ensconced in the discipline's traditional paradigms that reflect and reproduce the settler-colonial ideology that legitimized their elite university status to begin with. We may call on our students and colleagues to "commit sociology," but which sociology are we committing?

However, it is in this moment of decolonization that we face a radical choice. Even as sociologists pursue decolonization, the works of DuBois, Addams, and so many other women and scholars of color become themselves *colonized* as sociologists while their radical activism becomes depoliticized. In other words, in an act of academic "diversity and inclusion," nonwhite male sociologists are welcomed into the canon of sociology but the more radical elements of their work—their activist engagement with revolutionary social justice organizing and movements—disappear. For example, Jane Addams becomes a progenitor of service learning, civic engagement, and community-based research instead of a socialist, radical union organizer, and anti-imperialist, antiwar activist (Harkavy and Puckett, 1994; Deegan, 2013; Daynes and Longo, 2004; Schneiderhan, 2011; Lengermann and Niebrugge, 2016). Du Bois is rightfully exalted for his groundbreaking sociological studies, such as the "Philadelphia Negro," and the development of the Atlanta School of Sociology (Hunter, 2015; Morris, 2015; Sall and Khan, 2017; Wright, 2017). Yet, as John Stanfield and others have argued, the turn toward communism and Pan-Africanism of Du Bois demonstrated a scholarship and activism framed by, and ensconced in, a struggle *against* colonialism, white supremacy, and imperialism, and *for* a "culturally inclusive global human rights" (Stanfield, 2010; see also Itzigsohn, 2013; Kelley, 1999). Too often, this latter Du Bois disappears as the more acceptable Du Bois takes his place in the sociological canon.

Decolonizing sociology must include moving away from the cynical inclusion of nonwhite, nonmale sociologists into the already colonized discipline and its neoliberal corporate functions. Instead, it should be a moment of revolutionary vision—an opportunity to create a sociology of hope. It should be an intellectual and engaged practice driven not by institutional professionalism and status, but by the work of linking our intellectual tools to the local and global struggles for liberation and justice. Such roots are available within the discipline, both from the Marxist tradition (Karl Marx, Antonio Gramsci, and Rosa Luxemburg) and from the Black Radical tradition (C.L.R James, Amilcar Cabral, Frantz Fanon, DuBois, and Wells). An increasingly decolonized sociology might also look to the Latin American roots of revolutionary social science, such as Carlos Mariategui, Orlando Fals Borda, and Paulo Freire, or Asian radicals, such as Bhikaiji Cama, Qui Jin, and Ho Chi Minh. The key distinction for a sociology of hope is its focus not on the *discipline* of sociology, but on an action-driven knowledge production for liberation.

Committing sociology within a radical action paradigm builds on the great sociological tradition of revolutionary thinkers who disparaged the myth of objective and neutral research. As Oliver Cromwell Cox (1948) argued, the sociologist should be "passionately partisan in favor of the welfare of the people and against the interest of the few when they seem to submerge that welfare.... the reason for the existence of the social scientist is that his academic findings contribute to the betterment of the people's well-being." However, to make such contributions requires that we make connections to local communities and global organizations, and infuse our sociological practice with the work of social change. In Chapter 2 of this volume, Adelman and Byard make it clear that the transnational lesbian, gay, bisexual, transgender, and queer (LGBTQ+) movement is driving the research and collaboration of NGOs, activists, and intellectuals, and "this combination of research and advocacy has led intergovernmental organizations, such as the UN, to encourage states to acknowledge and protect LGBTQ+

youth." Increasingly, engaged scholars and activists are finding myriad ways to go beyond providing information and analysis to impact organizing, mobilization, and empowerment.

Our sociological theory will be, as it always has been, inspired and informed by struggles over: working conditions, human health, and dignity; land use, land rights, and human rights; and the power to determine public policy and economic and global security. We need to ask questions not only about the social relevance of our research, but also about how such work should be used to implement the movements and policies we propose and support and engage with.

References

August, A. (2014) Commit sociology. *The Society Pages*, August 6. Available at: www.thesocietypages.org/clippings/2014/09/06/now-is-the-time-for-canada-to-commit-sociology/

Bellah, R.N., Madsen, R. Sullivan, W.M. Swidler, A., and Tipton, S.M. (2007) *Habits of the Heart, With a New Preface: Individualism and Commitment in American Life*. Berkeley, CA: University of California Press.

Benjamin, W. (1986) *Illuminations*. Random House Digital, Inc, 241(2).

Black, T. and Dolgon, C. (2021) Zombie sociology: why our discipline is so susceptible to the undead. *Critical Sociology*, 47(3): 507–14.

Brym, B. and Ramos, H. (2013) Actually, now is the perfect time to "commit sociology." *Scatterplot: The Unruly Darings of Public Sociology*, April 25. Available at: http://projects.chass.utoronto.ca/brym/commit.htm.

Cox, O.C. (1948) *Caste, Class, and Race: A Study in Social Dynamics*, New York, NY: Monthly Review Press.

Daynes, G. and Longo, N.V. (2004) Jane Addams and the origins of service-learning practice in the United States. *Michigan Journal of Community Service Learning*, 11(1): 5–13.

Deegan, M.J. (2013) Jane Addams, the Hull-House school of sociology, and social justice, 1892 to 1935. *Humanity & Society*, 37(3): 248–58.

Dolgon, C. (2013) Now's the time: committing sociology in the new world. *Baddass Sociologist*, Summer.

Dolgon, C. (2015) *Kill It to Save It: An Autopsy of Capitalism's Triumph over Democracy*. Bristol: Policy Press.

Doucet, A. and Siltanen, J. (2017) Committing sociology: methodological and epistemological reflections introduction. *Canadian Review of Sociology*, 54(3): 360–3.

Fitzpatrick, M. (2013) Harper on terror arrests: not a time for "sociology." *CBC News*, April 25. Available at: www.cbc.ca/news/politics/harper-on-terror-arrests-not-a-time-for-sociology-1.1413502

Harkavy, I. and Puckett, J.L. (1994) Lessons from Hull House for the contemporary urban university. *Social Service Review*, 68(3): 299–321.

Hunter, M.A. (2015) WEB Du Bois and black heterogeneity: how the Philadelphia negro shaped American sociology. *The American Sociologist*, 46(2): 219–33.

Itzigsohn, J. (2013) Class, race, and emancipation: the contributions of the black Jacobins and black reconstruction in America to historical sociology and social theory. *The CLR James Journal*, 19(1/2): 177–98.

Jones, C. (2015) Penal populism: the politicization of crime under Harper. *Policy Options*, December 4.

Kelley, R.D.G. (1999) "But a local phase of a world problem": black history's global vision, 1883–1950. *The Journal of American History*, 86(3): 1045–77.

Knudson, S. and Hahn, D. (2020) *Committing Sociology: Critical Perspectives on our Social World*. Toronto: Pearson Canada.

Lengermann, P.M. and Niebrugge, G. (2016) Scholarship and advocacy: continuing the feminist revision of sociology's history. *Contemporary Sociology*, 45(5): 558–62.

Matthews, R. (2014) Committing Canadian sociology: developing a Canadian sociology and a sociology of Canada. *Canadian Review of Sociology/Revue canadienne de sociologie*, 51(2): 107–27.

Morris, A. (2015) *The Scholar Denied*. Berkeley, CA: University of California Press.

National Post (2013) String of terror incidents no reason to "commit sociology": Stephen Harper. April 25. Available at: https://nationalpost.com/news/politics/string-of-terror-incidents-no-reason-to-commit-sociology-stephen-harper

Newburn, T. and Jones, T. (2005) Symbolic politics and penal populism: the long shadow of Willie Horton. *Crime, Media, Culture*, 1(1): 72–87.

Pratt, J. (2007) *Penal Populism*. New York, NY: Routledge.

Sall, D. and Khan, S. (2017) What elite theory should have learned, and can still learn, from W.E.B. DuBois. *Ethnic & Racial Studies*, 40(3): 512–14.

Schneiderhan, E. (2011) Pragmatism and empirical sociology: the case of Jane Addams and Hull-House, 1889–1895. *Theory and Society*, 40(6): 589–617.

Spalter-Roth, R., Best, A.L., and White, P.E. (2018) Bringing sociology into the public policy process: a relational network approach. *The American Sociologist*, 49: 434–47.

Stanfield, J.H. (2010) Du Bois on citizenship: revising the "Du Bois as sociologist" canon. *Journal of Classical Sociology*, 10(3): 171–88.

The Sociological Post (2020) On committing acts of sociology. October 11. Available at: http://theradicalsociologicalpost.wordpress.com/2020/10/?msclkid=1ce48a50afca11eca618e7a80ef8d211

Wright, E., II (2017) *The First American School of Sociology: WEB Du Bois and the Atlanta Sociological Laboratory*. New York, NY: Routledge.

Wynn, J. (2013) Commit sociology. *Everyday Sociology*, May 1. Available at: http://www.everydaysociologyblog.com/jonanthan-wynn/page/9/?ms clkid=9a5dbd56afca11ec93e3161baea8f928

Afterword

Héctor L. Delgado

From its inception, the *Agenda for Social Justice (Agenda)* was driven by a desire to make sociological research on pressing social problems (and solutions to these problems) more accessible, that is, to reach audiences other than sociologists, including (if not especially) elected officials and policymakers. The first issue of *Agenda* in 2004 was a "report" sent to members of Congress, governors, large-city mayors, major newspapers, and public policy centers. However, as painstaking as the research on social problems is, it pales by comparison to the task of getting elected officials and policymakers to respond to excellent and accessible analyses of a wide range of problems. Unfortunately, while we wait for a response, these problems, and the pain and suffering they cause—disproportionately, and not coincidentally, to the most vulnerable and least powerful communities—persist. As a social justice organization (and for that moniker to have any meaning), we have to find ways to make a difference and to attach a sense of urgency to it that is commensurate with the levels of injustice that the research in these chapters reveal.

The politicization of problems has always complicated the task of finding and implementing fixes—but, perhaps, now more than ever. The politicization of the COVID-19 pandemic alone, despite compelling scientific medical evidence to guide us, has resulted in hundreds of thousands of unnecessary deaths and contributed enormously to an erosion in society's trust in and reliance on science. When science is ignored, superstition, greed, and intolerance gain traction, especially to the detriment of the poor, disproportionately people of color, and, internationally, to the detriment of the Global South. We are now witnessing the rapid rise of white supremacy and authoritarianism in the world, including in the US, where state legislatures are passing laws designed to suppress the vote of racialized people. This attack on democracy may be the most pressing social problem facing the country. Once again, we—as sociologists, as a discipline, as a social justice organization, and as participants in a social justice movement—have to find a way to participate much more meaningfully in the public discourse on these problems.

A good place to begin is to ask why we and the discipline have been relatively absent in the public arena. It is not as unusual to see articles in popular magazines, like *The Atlantic* and *The Nation*, or appearances on news programs like CNN by historians, psychologists, and economists as it is to see the same by sociologists. Publishing in non-academic publications, including Op-Eds in newspapers (training on which the Society for the Study of Social Problems [SSSP] is now offering members), and appearing on television news programs are potential outlets for sociological research and perspectives. Individuals can, and should, join social action organizations like Black Lives Matter (BLM), run for elective office *at every level*, and in other ways contribute to conversations that take place outside of academia. How much of a presence do sociologists, for example, have in the nation's capital? Neil Irwin (2017), a chief economics correspondent for the *New York Times*, asked in 2017: "What if sociologists had as much influence as economists?" "Walk half a city block in downtown Washington," he wrote, "and there is a good chance that you will pass an economist" (Irwin, 2017). The same cannot be said of sociologists. Irwin observed, if not lamented, that while sociology did not have the ear of presidents, the discipline "may actually do a better job of explaining what has gone wrong in large swaths of the United States and other advanced nations in recent years" (Irwin, 2017). Neither Irwin nor I have to convince anyone reading this afterword that the discipline has a great deal to offer to conversations on social problems, beginning with how we think about social problems.

Asking, as sociologists do, how or why some social phenomena are deemed social problems while others are not, contributes immediately a critical dimension to any discussion on social problems. According to Heiner (2013: 3), for example, a social problem is "a phenomenon regarded as bad or undesirable by a significant number of people or a number of significant people who mobilize to remedy it." A group of *more* significant people can, of course, prevent not only the remedy, but also whether the phenomenon even constitutes a social problem. Voting rights is a case in point. Opposition to a recent voting rights bill (as a response to attempts to suppress the racialized vote) was based principally on the assertion that racism was no longer a problem in the electoral process. After all, did we not elect a black man as president of the US? Did South Carolinians not elect a black man as Senator? And did the Supreme Court in *Shelby County v. Holder* (570 U.S. 529 [2013]) not hold nearly a decade ago that the coverage formula in Section 4(b) of the Voting Rights Act was unconstitutional? (This decision all but invited states to pass the restrictive voting laws we are seeing today.) It does not matter whether any of these assertions are true. All that the opponents of voting rights legislation needed was 41 "significant" people to kill it; they got 52. For many, ensuring voting rights for everyone is the goal; for others, the goal is to deny it to some.

The process of what constitutes a social problem and what remedies are acceptable clearly is a political one, and certainly not one that is value-free (Eitzen and Zinn, 2000). In one of the earliest, and most influential, books on social problems, Spector and Kitsuse (1987: 21) observed that "the activities through which definitions of social problems are constructed are as observable through sociological research techniques as are any of the phenomena that occupy the attention of social scientists." It is precisely this kind of research that the authors in this volume and other social problems scholars are conducting. It is work that finds, time and time again, enormous economic, political, and social inequalities, and power differentials, at the root of virtually every social problem. Anything short of changing this power differential amounts to a Band-Aid. In a chapter on workers and the workplace in an edited volume on social problems, I argued that if "workers and others to whom neoliberalism has not been very kind do not organize effectively to improve conditions of work, to redistribute income and wealth more equitably, and to protect the environment, change—certainly significant change—is not likely to occur" (Delgado, 2018: 546). This requires a social justice movement that transcends borders of every kind.

Perhaps social justice activists can take a page from the neoliberalism playbook. Neoliberal forces have succeeded where social justice forces have not. In the US, they control a majority of state legislatures and governors' mansions, have seized control of the Supreme Court (and, in effect, have converted it into another legislative branch), and may be poised to retake the House and Senate in 2022, as well as possibly the White House in 2024. (Neoliberalism has not ignored local school boards either, where whether to teach students about the country's racist history is actually contested.) None of this happened accidentally or overnight. It was, and continues to be, a well-planned, well-executed, disciplined effort, executed with a sense of resolve bordering on survival (the survival of white supremacy) that progressive forces in this country have not been able to emulate. It is sometimes characterized as progressives bringing a knife to a gunfight.

The struggle for social justice will require the same patience and coordinated action adopted and exhibited by neoliberals. It will have to be a movement of different progressive forces, including other progressive social science organizations. To make the challenge more daunting, since 2017, 20 state legislatures have enacted 36 laws penalizing, even criminalizing, different forms of protest activities, with 25 others contemplating similar bills, and in Florida, the governor is proposing the creation of a security force to police voting (see Halliday and Hanna, 2021). This requires us to identify what we can—and cannot—do as an organization. We cannot, for example, do what BLM does. However, we may be able to assist BLM to do what it does. While problems often require short-term solutions to address the immediate suffering of millions, long-term solutions to these problems require fundamental social-structural changes in the distribution of wealth and power, recognizing (as Jerry Jacobs and Elinore Avni underscore in this volume) that an understanding and resolution of these problems benefit immeasurably from, if not *require*, an international perspective.

References

Delgado, H.L. (2018) Problems of the workplace and workforce. In A. Javier Treviño (ed) *The Cambridge Handbook of Social Problems* (vol 1). Cambridge: Cambridge University Press, pp 531–49.

Eitzen, D.S. and Zinn, M.B. (2000) *Social Problems*. Boston, MA: Allyn and Bacon.

Halliday, E. and Hanna, R. (2021) State anti-protest laws and their constitutional implications. *Lawfare*, March 25. Available at: www.lawfareblog.com/state-anti-protest-laws-and-their-constitutional-implications

Heiner, R. (2013) *Social Problems: An Introduction to Critical Constructionism*. New York, NY: Oxford University Press.

Irwin, N. (2017) What if sociologists had as much influence as economists? *New York Times*, March 17. Available at: www.nytimes.com/2017/03/17/upshot/what-if-sociologists-had-as-much-influence-as-economists.html

Spector, M. and Kitsuse, J.I. (1987) *Constructing Social Problems*. Hawthorne, NY: Aldine de Gruyter.